FRIENDSHIP
WITH
GOD

Books
By Wayne Monbleau

Lessons In Life For The 21st Century
From The Solitude Of Jesus

You Don't Find Water On The Mountaintop -
Discovering Nourishment In Life's Valleys

Living In Love -
Real Values For A Relevant Faith

Grace: The Essence Of God

Friendship With God

Edited by Wayne Monbleau
The Odes Of Solomon

Booklets
By Wayne Monbleau

Behold I Do Something New

Love One Another

A New Life In Jesus' Own Words

Wayne Monbleau

FRIENDSHIP
WITH
GOD

Loving Grace Publications

Loving Grace Publications
P.O. Box 500, Lafayette, New Jersey 07848
1-800-480-1638
www.lovinggrace.org   email:loving@lovinggrace.org

ISBN: 0-944648-62-2
Library of Congress Control Number: 2002095771

First Printing: April, 1982
Second Printing: November, 1982
Third Printing: June, 1984
Fourth Printing: March, 1986
Fifth Printing: August, 1987
Sixth Printing, September, 1990
Seventh Printing, December, 2002, Revised Edition

Cover Art: Patti Sullivan
Author Photograph: Vincent Nicoletti

Unless otherwise noted, Scripture quotations are from the NEW
AMERICAN STANDARD BIBLE, ©1960, 1962, 1963, 1968, 1971,
1972, 1973, 1975, 1977, by The Lockman Foundation.
Used by permission.

Printed in Canada

CONTENTS

Preface
To The 2002 Edition
ix

Introduction
1

Chapter One
Appreciating Friendship
5

Chapter Two
Establishing Friendship: Abraham And Grace
29

Chapter Three
Hearing Your Friend
51

Chapter Four
The Blessings Of Hearing Your Friend
71

Chapter Five
Protecting Your Friendship
89

Chapter Six
Loyalty
119

To my Best Friend.

PREFACE TO THE 2002 REVISED EDITION

A little more than twenty years ago I set out to write a book that would, hopefully, express the joy, peace, stability and enlightenment found in the realization of an intimate friendship with God. The world has changed so much in these past two decades. Yet this simple, wonderful friendship with God continues to beat within, growing, deepening, and holding me forever together in the heart of my Savior. I am more grateful now than ever for my friendship with God.

When the sixth printing of *Friendship With God* was running out, I felt this would be a good time to clean up a few typographical errors I was aware of, and to also reset the book in a more pleasing typeface. This we have done.

But, of course, things got a bit more involved. While the main text of *Friendship With God* remains unchanged, I have added a few more thoughts and Scriptures, and have lightly reworded certain sections, in the hope of making even more clear and desirable this life-enhancing gift which God graciously offers us in Himself. As I have spent the past few weeks going over this manuscript my own gratitude has only grown to my Abba Father that He has given us His Son to be our *"Friend that sticks closer than a brother" (Proverbs 18:24)*. I am happy to say that friendship with God has gloriously stood the true test of time.

I wish to thank Patti Sullivan for her original cover drawing. I also thank my wife (and best friend next to Jesus), Debbie Monbleau, and Judith Lopez, who have helped immeasurably in this project with their own editorial readings and suggestions. My deep appreciation and thanks also go to the board of directors and staff of Loving Grace Ministries, true partners in spirit and in ministry. And to the thousands who have been blessed through reading and realizing their own Friendship with God, and who have helped to spread this simple message around the world; may God continue to reveal even more of Himself to us all, that we may always be growing in this dynamic forever-friendship.

In closing, let me share the same parting words the apostle John expressed, as he concluded his final letter to the church of Jesus Christ. Speaking of his understanding of our identity as Christians, John wrote, *"Peace be to you. The friends greet you. Greet the friends by name" (3rd John 1:15)*. May God reveal Himself to you, greeting you afresh as His *"friends by name"* through these pages and may He give you a new revelation of yourself as His Own dearly beloved friend.

In Him,

Rev. Wayne Monbleau
Sparta, New Jersey
October 20, 2002

INTRODUCTION

Friendship with God. In the past, I had read books and had heard people speak of someone being a friend of God as if that person had arrived at a place of super spirituality which only a few of God's choicest children ever see. Being a friend of God, in their words, was a mystical and awesome experience that, apparently, the average Christian could never hope to attain. I would read these books, and hear these people, desiring the intimate relationship being spoken of. But, at the same time I was saddened, thinking I would probably never know that special closeness with the Lord.

All that has changed. I've discovered the Bible has a lot to say about our living in an intimate friendship with God. And the truth of the Scripture is this: whosoever will may come.

Entering into this simple realization has enabled me to personally know and experience the joyful fulfillment found in a friendship with God. This has produced and is continuing to produce in me the ability to see God's true nature, the blessing of recognizing my new creation nature in Jesus Christ, and I have an ever deepening appreciation for the finished work of Calvary.

In my counseling ministry I have talked with thousands of Christians who feel frustrated in their walk and growth in Christ. Usually this frustration, or even despair, is accompanied by a sense of distance between the individual and God. Feeling their performance isn't up to God's requirements, they assume God must not be pleased with them, hence the feeling of distance.

This is simply a case of placing the cart before the horse. Our performance does not determine God's attitude. The truth is that if we will realize God's loving attitude towards us, this will become the very thing that will radically and eternally change our walk from one of frustration to one of joyful growth and intimacy in the Lord.

This book is the fulfillment of a long-standing desire I've had to share with the body of Christ, and the world at large, the exciting discovery I've made concerning friendship with God. It's my prayer that these pages will enrich your life and bring you into the beautifully abundant experience of your being a friend with God.

Wayne Monbleau
September 23, 1981
Southwest Harbor, Maine

CHAPTER 1

APPRECIATING FRIENDSHIP

Are you God's friend?

What is your first thought in response to this question? Is it, "Oh, I wish I was"? Maybe your first thought is, "Yes, praise God, I am!" Or perhaps you're thinking, "No, I don't think I am."

Regardless of what your answer to my question is right now, it's my hope, prayer and expectation that by the time you finish reading this book, you will know without any doubt at all that you are God's friend. Not a casual acquaintance, but a true intimate friend.

Let me ask you another question. Is God your Friend? You may find it a little easier to say "yes" to this question. If you find yourself answering yes to my second question, but somehow not feeling so sure about the answer to my first question then this, in itself, is a strong indication that you need to have God minister to you regarding your friendship with Him. After all, it doesn't say much for a friendship if you are the one who considers the other your friend, but you don't experience a return in affection.

If you do consider God as your Friend and yet wonder if He looks upon you as His friend, I believe the truths from Scripture I am going to share with you in this book will bring you into a glorious new awareness of Christ as your Friend, and you as His friend. And I maintain this, <u>you are God's best friend!</u>

"There is a friend who sticks closer than a brother" (Proverbs 18:24). This is the type of friendship God desires you to realize in your relationship with Him. And, as you come into this realization of God's commitment of friendship to you, you will find yourself experiencing new strength and purpose as a Christian.

Sometimes we can fall into a trap of keeping God at arm's length. We may think God is so big and powerful that He couldn't be bothered with us. So, we may go to church, participate in Christian service and, basically, think that's all there is to it. This is a trap. It's the trap of "God's so big and I'm so small." Why is this type of thinking a trap? Because it keeps us from drawing near to the Lord to know Him in an intimate way.

It's also a trap because it deprives God of His joy. He wants to have an intimate friendship with you. He desires for you to draw near to Him. Scripture says, *"Draw near to God and He will draw near to you"(James 4:8)*. As you open your heart up to the possibility of being God's best friend, you will actually be making His joy complete. Does this sound hard to believe?

I have come to know this truth as reality in my own life and, all I can say is, having God as my Best Friend and knowing I am His best friend has made my Christian walk an absolute delight. I now know Jesus Christ as my *"Friend who sticks closer than a brother."*

Let me share something with you from Scripture which speaks about our friendship with God. In the Gospel of John, Chapter 15, Jesus said, *"Greater love has no one than this, that one lay down his life for his friends. You are My friends, if you do what I command you. No longer do I call you slaves; for the slave does not know what his master is doing; but I have called you friends, for all things that I have heard from My Father I have made known to you. You did not choose Me, but I chose you, and appointed you, that you should go and bear fruit, and that your fruit should remain, that whatever you ask of the Father in My name, He may give to you. This I command you, that you love one another"*

(Verses 13-17).

"*No longer do I call you slaves . . . but I have called you friends.*" What does Jesus call us? Friends. It seems pretty clear to me in this Scripture that Jesus was emphasizing the fact that He considers us as friends. He wanted to make it plain to His disciples that they were not slaves. He thought of them as His friends. Hopefully, this will become plain to you as well.

I would like to share six things with you from these verses that your friendship with God will enable you to more fully appreciate in your life.

Do you have trouble appreciating what you have in Christ? Perhaps you hear people talking about the riches that are yours in Christ. Yet, in your own life, you may have a difficult time seeing these riches. Well, if you will let the idea of your being a friend with God sink in, I believe you will be able to more readily understand and appropriate God's riches for yourself.

So, just from these verses, I want to show you six truths that you will be able to have a new and growing appreciation of as you let God minister His friendship to you.

APPRECIATING
CHRIST'S DEATH FOR YOU

This first truth is found in the 13th verse

of John 15: *"Greater love has no one than this, that one lay down his life for his friends."* Why do you suppose Jesus made this statement? This verse shows our Savior telling His disciples two things. First, He was telling them He was going to die for them. Secondly, He was revealing His motivation to them.

It's one thing to acknowledge Jesus died for you. It's quite another thing to understand why He died for you. To know the former and not the latter is to cheat yourself of the love of God. According to this verse, why did Jesus die for you, for me, for everyone? Love! The greatest love. Remember, Scripture says, *"Greater love has no one than this."* When Jesus was crucified at Calvary, shedding His blood for our sins, this was the greatest expression of love mankind would ever witness. Jesus Himself said that He couldn't show us His love in any greater way than to lay down His life for us.

And, in this 13th verse, what does Jesus refer to us as? His friends. It's true to say Jesus died for the sins of the world, but don't let yourself ever forget that Jesus died for individuals. He died for you. Remember the "God's so big and I'm so small" trap I mentioned earlier? We can have a tendency to think that, in God's eyes, we are just some faceless number; a statistic. This is simply not true. Jesus would never have called you friend if that were His attitude. The very fact of His calling you His friend tells me that He had you, personally, in His mind when He suffered at Calvary. It's true. God saw you as an individual, a unique person, a personal friend, and this is why He went to the cross.

The Apostle Paul wrote to the Ephesians, *"He chose us in Him before the foundation of the world" (Ephesians 1:4).* Now that's forethought! Think about that. Before the foundation of the world you were chosen. Long before you existed, God knew who you were and had you in His heart. So, when Jesus referred to His friends in John 15:13, He had you in mind. He already knew you and called you friend. Don't you want to know this kind of friendship?

To think of God having such a deep and abiding love for us is amazing. That is exactly why I'm sharing this with you. God's love is deeper than anything we could ever imagine. Once again, in his letter to the Ephesian church, Paul spoke of *"the love of Christ, which surpasses knowledge" (Ephesians 3:19).* If you were to give every moment of your life over to seeing and meditating upon the love of Christ, there would still be unfathomable riches you wouldn't have even touched upon.

"Greater love has no one than this, that one lay down His life for His friends." As you begin to allow God to minister His friendship to you,

you will have an ever deepening appreciation for the death of Christ for you. His supreme love was revealed in His sacrifice. If you will believe what this Scripture says, you will grow in the understanding of that love. However, if you continue to see yourself as some stranger to God or, at best, as just one unimportant soul among the multitudes, then it's quite possible you will never truly see God's love for you in the death of Christ. It's in realizing you are the friend being spoken of in this verse that your horizons will expand concerning an ever-increasing appreciation of the death of your Savior for you.

APPRECIATING
GOD'S LOVE

In the 14th Verse of this section from John 15 Jesus said, *"You are My friends if you do what I command you."* And what is it He commands us? The answer is found in the 17th verse. *"This I command you, that you love one another."* Some may misinterpret verse 14 to mean it's only when we are obeying commandments that God looks upon us as His friend. That would be a conditional friendship, wouldn't it?

First we need to see what His commandment is and, as verse 17 tells us, it's love. Put verses 14 and 17 together and it would be, "You are my friends if you love one another."

We have already seen that long before we were created God saw us as His friends. In other words, God established our friendship with Him before we had the ability to love one another. So, does this verse mean that God is now placing conditions upon this friendship?

Let's look a little deeper into this. What is the heart of true friendship? Love. It's as we love that we prove ourselves to be friends. We are in the act of friendship, or the realization of friendship, as we love. Love is the very essence of God's friendship with us.

How is it that we become God's friend? Is this something we have originated? No, He did it. He loved us. He died for us, and He initiated friendship with us. In his letter to the church at Rome, Paul wrote, *"God demonstrates His own love toward us, in that while we were yet sinners, Christ died for us" (Romans 5:8).* You see, God didn't wait for some sign on our part before He loved us. It was *"while we were yet sinners,* [that] *Christ died for us."* God's love has established our relationship with Him. And how does this take effect in our lives? By receiving. It's when we receive Jesus Christ as our personal Savior and Lord that we are born again. And, it's as we receive the love of God that we are able to realize our friendship with Him.

So, as we love one another we are placing ourselves in the best position to know the love

which Christ has for us. Thus we can understand our friendship with God. *"You are My
friends if you do what I command you."* - *"This I
command you, that you love one another."* We
allow the reality of our friendship with God to
shine forth as we love. Why? Because any love
that we express is a result of our having first
been loved by Him. First John says, *"We love,
because He first loved us" (4:19).* When we love,
we more freely enable ourselves to know God
as our Friend. And, it is by seeing ourselves as
God's friends that we are able to love.

Our friendship with God is based upon a
communication of love. God wants to communicate His love to you right now because you
are His friend. He wants you to know Him
intimately, just as best friends know each other
better than anybody else. If you never love,
then you may not be receiving God's love on a
daily basis. By not receiving God's love, this
may keep you from knowing this great friendship I am speaking of.

Love is the heart of friendship, and you will
be able to appreciate the love of God in a much
greater way as you allow your friendship with
Him to develop. It's by love that friendship is
established, and it's by love that friendship
grows. How exciting it is to know that you will
actually have the privilege of discovering new
facets of God's love, each day, as you walk in

13

this friendship.

Have you ever heard someone say, "I never really knew what love was until I met so and so"? I hope you will soon be able to make this same exclamation about your life in Christ. Jesus said the greatest commandment is to love. How sad it is that many Christians can spend a lifetime in the Lord and yet have such a meager understanding of His love. My own realization of my friendship with God makes me aware of His love like nothing else ever has. Every day provides a new opportunity to see more of this *"love of Christ, which surpasses knowledge" (Ephesians 3:19)*. You can definitely expect to have an ever-increasing appreciation of God's love as you develop your friendship with God.

APPRECIATING
CHRISTIAN SERVICE

A third item you will be able to appreciate is found in John 15:15. *"No longer do I call you slaves; for the slave does not know what his master is doing; but I have called you friends, for all things that I have heard from My Father I have made known to you."*

How do you see yourself as you serve God? Are you a slave, or are you a friend? Do you know the difference between these two terms?

There's a big difference between being a slave and being a friend. If you are a slave, then you do something because you have to. There's no relationship in it at all. You are told to do something and you have to do it. It's that cut-and-dried. And, when you follow orders, you don't get any thanks. You don't receive any blessing. But, if you are a friend, you do something because you want to. You see how you can please your friend by your service, and you know your friend will rejoice and be thankful. You are motivated by love. You are blessed as you serve. It's not a question of having to do something as a slave. It's a matter of doing something because it's a joy for you to do it as a friend. As a friend, you realize you are in a love relationship.

When you read Scripture, do you say to yourself, "Well, the Bible says this is what I must do, so I guess I'd better do it"? If that is what you say, then I must tell you, you are seeing yourself as a slave. That is tragic, because Jesus specifically says you are not a slave, but a friend.

As a friend, reading Scripture becomes a delight, for you know you'll be in blessed communion, being fed and nourished by your Friend's words. Friendship with God removes a feeling of boredom and an unhealthy fear of God from reading the Word of God. Instead of feeling disconnected from Scripture, as a friend you'll be able to joyfully declare with the Psalm-ist, *"Your word is a lamp to my feet and a light to my path"* (Psalm 119:105).

It is so sad to see a Christian who has a slave mentality rather than a friendship mentality. Jesus said, *"The slave does not know what his master is doing."* If you walk through each day carrying about this slave mentality, then you won't know what the Lord is doing. Do you want to know what God is doing? Don't you want to be seeing Him as you serve? Do you ever complain about never knowing what God is up to in your own life? Do you feel as though the parade has passed you by? If you do feel this way, then ask yourself this question: "What is my mentality?"

With a slave, service is drudgery. With a friend, service is a joy. *"I have called you friends, for all things that I have heard from My Father I have made known to you."* When you realize you are God's friend, serving Him is great because you know, as you obey Him, He will be revealing all things to you. You can see your service as a chance to express your love right back to your Savior.

It's much better to serve God as a friend. When you are a friend, you know the true nature of the One you are a friend with, and you will do something for your Friend because you love your Friend. You will experience the healthy blessing of a true motivation and desire in your service to God as you look upon it as friendship. However, if you continue with a slave mentality, then your motivation may more likely be fear. You will serve God, but you may do it out of fear. You may be afraid that if you don't serve Him, He might do something terrible to you, or you'll carry a fear in your heart that God won't love you as much unless you're serving Him.

The choice is up to you. Jesus has certainly made His attitude clear regarding your serving Him. But, the decision is yours. You can serve as a slave and be full of fear and misery, feeling distant from the presence of God. Or you can serve as a friend, being absolutely delighted as you serve. Which will you choose? If you do choose to serve as a friend, then you will have a whole new appreciation for Christian service. Remember, Jesus calls you a friend, not a slave. So please don't think He wants you to be a slave. He wants a friend.

APPRECIATING
CONFIDENCE IN GOD

A fourth thing you will be able to appreciate is also found in John 15:15. It's in the phrase, *"All things I have heard from my Father I have made known to you."*

I conduct a live call-in counseling radio program, "Let's Talk About Jesus," which I currently host six days a week, an hour a day. People call in for prayer and counsel from Scripture. Countless lives have been changed over the years through this radio ministry and I thank God for letting me take part in this outreach. As I have counseled with literally thousands, I have noticed one particular recurring complaint among Christians. They say, "I'm going through an awful trial, and God isn't telling me why this is happening. I go to Him in prayer, but I feel like He's not even listening." Have you ever said this? If we are honest, I think we can all confess to having had that feeling at one time or another. But, if this is the norm for you, then something is wrong. If you always feel distant from God, and if you always feel like He's not telling you anything, then there is definitely a communication gap somewhere.

It is so important to realize your friendship with God when you feel this way. Very often, what will happen is this: some trial falls upon you and you immediately become full of worry. You think, "What have I done wrong?" You ask God to tell you what is happening and you don't get a reply right away. So, you begin to feel like He has left you. Then you start digging around inside of yourself, trying to locate some "secret sin" that might be the cause of your troubles. As you do that, you develop a total sin and failure awareness. Down and down you go, on a spiral that brings you ever further into despair.

I tell you, in the Name of the Lord, this does not need to happen. This entire downward spiral is a result of a poor comprehension of your friendship with God. If you ignore Jesus as your Friend, then you place yourself in a situation of thinking God has abandoned you. And that's just about the worst thing you can do when you are going through a trial. It is in our trials that we need, more than ever, to see our great friendship with God. It's when we face difficulty that we can benefit the most from being aware of our relationship with our Lord.

If you know God is your Friend, and you are His friend, then the Word of the Lord will be real to you. You won't feel like He has left you. You will know and will be able to confess God's promise where He said, *"I will never desert you, nor will I ever forsake you" (Hebrews 13:5)*. Isaiah's words will be your confidence: *"When you pass through the waters, I will be with you; and through the rivers, they will not overflow you. When you walk through the fire, you will not be scorched, nor will the flame burn you. For I am the Lord your God, . . . since you are precious in My sight, since you are honored and I love you" (Isaiah 43:2-4)*. Instead of being in a time where you feel far away from God, you will be able to have a time of special closeness to the Lord. In fact, you may discover a new depth to your friendship with God that you never before knew existed.

"All things I have heard from My Father, I have made known to you." If you will consider your friendship with God when you go through a trial, you will know everything is in His hands. Instead of saying, "Why won't you tell me what's going on," you will know He will tell you all things in His time. You will also have a complete assurance about entrusting yourself fully to His care. Instead of being overwhelmed by worry, you will be able to have His peace which passes understanding *(Philippians 4:7)*. Instead of diving into your faults, sins, and failures, you will be able to feast upon His goodness. You will know the truth that King David wrote about so long ago, *"In the day of trouble He will conceal me in His tabernacle; in the secret place of His tent He will hide me; He will lift me up on a rock, and now my head will be lifted up above my enemies around me, and I will offer in His tent sacrifices with shouts of joy; I will sing, yes I will sing praises to the Lord"* *(Psalm 27: 5-6)*.

As we walk with God in friendship, He will make all things known to us. This will produce in us a confidence in His Word. We will learn to relate to what He says rather than to what we feel, and we can expect to grow progressively as we abide in Him. Jesus will make things known to us on a continuing basis. So, another great thing you will be able to appreciate in your friendship with God is the growing confidence you will have in Him.

APPRECIATING
SALVATION

John 15:16 declares one of the greatest truths from God's Word, *"You did not choose Me, but I chose you."*

I touched upon this subject briefly when we were seeing how our friendship with God gives us a deeper appreciation for the death of Christ. I shared the Scripture with you which says we were chosen before the foundation of the world. I would like to take another look now at this matter of our being chosen by God.

We often think of our salvation as a matter of our choosing to accept the Lord. And indeed, that is what we do. We make a conscious decision to receive Jesus Christ.

And yet, Jesus said, *"You did not choose Me, but I chose you."* At this point you may say, "But I'm the one who did the choosing. I'm the one who accepted Christ." All this is true, but it's not the whole truth.

When you first came to Christ to be born again, do you realize that what was really happening was that God had chosen you? Can you imagine, God was caring for you so much that all your life, through the mountains and the valleys, He had been slowly but surely drawing you to the place where you would finally receive Him? God did all that could be done in order for you to know Him. He made the way of salvation clear.

So much of religion tells us what we must do in order to find God. Christianity is just the opposite. Christianity tells us what God has done so He can find us. Christianity is God reaching His hand out to mankind through the death and resurrection of Jesus Christ. When you accept His hand, it's not so much your choosing God as it is His choosing you.

God wanted to be friends with you so much, *"that He gave His only begotten Son, that whoever believes in Him should not perish, but have eternal life" (John 3:16).* At the moment of your salvation, you were actually fulfilling God's desire. Have you ever seen your salvation in this light?

I remember when the Lord showed me the true meaning of a certain Scripture. In the 15th chapter of Luke's Gospel, verse 10 says, *"There is joy in the presence of the angels of God over one sinner who repents."* I was looking at this Scripture one day and I felt God, through His still small inner voice, say to me, "Do you know why the angels rejoice?" I had my ideas but I figured He was trying to make a point to me.

So I replied that I did not know, and asked why the angels rejoice. The answer was very simple: "The angels rejoice because they see Me rejoicing." At that moment I could just see the Lord with a beaming countenance, in sheer delight over just one soul coming to Him. I could see His heart's desire being met. This is why I say, when you come to the Lord for salvation, you are fulfilling His desire.

So, yet another truth you will be able to appreciate through your friendship with God is your salvation. I thank God every day for my salvation. The more I grow in Him, the more I thank Him. My salvation means more to me at this moment than it has ever meant. To think that through all my life, God had been patiently bringing me to Himself by His Spirit is almost more than I can comprehend. I can look back now in the years that I did not know Jesus as my Savior, and I can recognize times when God's hand was in my life, protecting me from something, or leading me in a particular way. Now that is friendship, when someone is your friend and you don't even know it.

<u>APPRECIATING</u>
<u>BEARING FRUIT</u>

The final point I would like to make from this portion of Scripture is found, once again, in John 15:16. *"You did not choose Me, but I*

23

chose you, and appointed you, that you should go and bear fruit, and that your fruit should remain."

Do you want to bear fruit? Do you want your life to be a reflection of Jesus Christ? In his second letter to the church at Corinth, Paul wrote, *"You are our letter, written in our hearts, known and read by all men" (3:2).* The Bible declares that the lives we live are letters to all men. So, what is our message to the world? If we live in a continuous state of frustration, then that will be our letter. If we are constantly fighting with God about who sits on the throne of our life, then that will be our letter. But, if we will walk in our friendship with God, rejoicing in the special relationship we have with Him, then that will be our letter to the world, and that will be the type of life that bears abundant fruit.

Can you grow yourself? Suppose you were a mustard seed. Let's say someone has planted you in rich soil, and they are taking care that you get just the right amount of water and sunshine. But you really want to grow. So, you clench your fists, grit your teeth, and say, "I will grow! Come on, grow! Grow! Grow!" And nothing happens. Why? Because the seed can't cause the growth by its own efforts. The seed has all it needs in it to grow, but the seed can't make itself grow. Now, that mustard seed has a choice. It can frantically try to grow itself, or it can rest secure in the gardener's care.

You are a seed; not a mustard seed, but an incorruptible seed *(I Peter 1:23)*. Because you are a seed, you have all you need for growth right inside of you. Unfortunately, many Christians do not understand this and as a result, they are like that mustard seed, all bound up in worry saying, "Grow, grow, grow!"

Well then, how do you grow? The answer is found in Paul's first epistle to the Corinthians. In the 7th verse of Chapter 3 the apostle wrote, *"So then neither the one who plants nor the one who waters is anything, but God who causes the growth."* There it is. God causes the growth. Can you grow yourself? No. Then how do you grow? By entrusting yourself to God. He causes the growth. If you drink in His Word every day, and bask in the sunshine of His love every day, you will certainly make it easier for God to grow you; but the growth itself comes from God.

There is a certain bus company whose motto is, "Leave the driving to us." I believe God has a motto concerning growth, "Leave the growing to Me."

Can you see what a blessing it is to realize that God is causing your growth? You don't need to carry that burden on your shoulders. All you need to do is to let God, your Heavenly Gardener, do His work in you.

Jesus said He has *"appointed you, that you*

should go and bear fruit." Instead of fretting over whether you will ever bear fruit or not, I encourage you to praise God that He <u>has</u> appointed you to bear fruit. There may be certain areas in your life where, presently, there may be no discernible fruit. But as you grow in your friendship with God, you will know you are in His hands and He will produce the fruit. Remember, the seed doesn't cause the growth; God does.

If you are always worrying about bearing fruit, then you must be trying to do God's job, because that is His responsibility. You just make sure you are in the good soil. Get plenty of water and sunshine, and God will take care of the fruit-bearing. It's as you walk in your friendship with God that you will be getting the best sunshine and watering.

"And your fruit should remain." God not only will grow you, and bear your fruit, but He will also make sure your fruit remains. How does all this seem to you? Do you get the feeling that there must be more to it for you to do? Well, perhaps you have just assumed this was your job for so long that it's hard for you to believe God loves you enough to do all this.

As I have shared these truths with you, I hope your eyes are opening up to the glorious friendship which is yours in Christ Jesus. In this chapter we have taken one basic section of

Scripture, John 15, verses 13-17. Dwelling upon your friendship with God, I have shared six wonderful truths that you will be able to understand and appreciate in a new and ever-increasing way as you are willing to believe you are God's friend. You will have a deepening gratitude for: Jesus' death for you, His love, Christian service, your confidence in God's Word, your salvation, and in your bearing fruit.

Friendship with God is the key which unlocks the door to living in a healthy and robust relationship with the Lord. Jesus is the one who has initiated this friendship. He laid down His life for you. He chose you. He did all that could be done in order to give you this friendship.

When you were growing up, perhaps you tried to make friends. Was there ever someone you wanted to be friends with more than any-one else? Maybe you gave them presents, or laughed extra hard at their jokes, or always made sure to try to do whatever they wanted. In this case, who would you say initiated the friend-ship? It was you. You made the first move.

Do you know this is exactly what God has done with you? He has given you His Son and He has made a joyfully abundant life possible. He has met your every eternal need. He has initiated this friendship.

I'm sure if a person ever showed you this

kind of love, you would gladly receive it. Well then, don't stand off from God's love. Don't say, "I don't deserve this" or "I can't accept this." Receive His love. Receive it all gladly and with thanksgiving.

Look at what God has done for you. In all of this He has said, "I love you, and I want to be your Friend." He knows all your faults and weaknesses, and He loves you anyway. He knows exactly what you are like, and He loves you.

Will you accept His friendship? If you are willing, then you will begin to appreciate your life in Christ in a deeper and more dynamic way than you have ever dreamed possible.

CHAPTER 2

ESTABLISHING FRIENDSHIP: ABRAHAM AND GRACE

"Abraham believed God, and it was reckoned to him as righteousness,' and he was called the friend of God." (James 2:23)

We have already beheld many wonderful aspects of our friendship with God. Through the Scriptures I've shared with you, I pray you are becoming absolutely convinced that this is exactly what God desires you to be experiencing in your daily walk with Him, Christ as your Best Friend and yourself as His best friend.

In this chapter I'd like to examine the process of how one becomes friends with God. We have seen that it is the Lord, Himself, who has initiated and made possible this intimate relationship. But, perhaps you might be thinking to yourself, "This sounds good, and I definitely want it, but how do I go about becoming God's friend? What must I do?" Maybe you're even thinking this sounds too good to be true, and couldn't possibly be as easy as I'm making it out to be.

If we are going to realize God's truth in our lives, we have to be willing to approach things His way and not our way. Our way often says, "Let me give you a hand, God" or "surely this will only happen through my obedience and efforts." However, God's way in this case, says, "Let Me do it all for I have done it all. Let Me give My friendship as a gift to you."

If you live in New York and want to drive to Canada, you don't head south for Florida. You follow the directions, and the directions in this example would lead you north to your destination. God's Word has directions, and we need to follow them. Don't fall into the trap of trying to earn this friendship that He has freely given you.

I want to share with you about the life of Abraham. Abraham was specifically called a friend of God, so let's see why and how he came to be called God's friend. As we do see this, I believe the way will appear more clearly than ever for you to understand how it is that you become God's friend.

In the second chapter of the Book of James, Scripture says, *"Abraham believed God, and it was* reckoned to him as righteousness,' and he was called the friend of God" (verse 23). The first line of this verse originally appears in the 15th chapter of Genesis. James quoted this Scripture in his letter and then added his own comment, "And he was called the friend of God." The prophet Isaiah also said Abraham was called God's friend (Isaiah 41:8).

Abraham seems to have been known for his friendship with God. Abraham was the father of the nation of Israel and, according to the books of Romans and Galatians, Abraham is the father of all those who come by faith to believe in Jesus Christ.

Why was Abraham called the friend of God? As we behold the answer to this question, we will also see how we can be known as the friends of God.

Abraham became a friend of God through belief. This was a faith friendship. "Abraham believed God, and it was reckoned to him as righteousness." This is the key phrase. In this chapter I will show you this verse in the four different places that it appears in the Bible. We have already seen this reference in the book of James, and I mentioned that it first appears in the Book of Genesis (15:6). There are two more places in the New Testament where the phrase "Abraham believed God, and it was reckoned to him as righteousness" appears. As we look at each of these instances, I believe you will clearly see how you can have this truth become powerfully effective in your own life.

Abraham's friendship with God was by faith and not by works. It was a gift and not something he achieved through his own efforts. It may seem to you that I am belaboring this point, and I am. For on this truth hangs not only your friendship with God, but your entire relationship with God as well. God has paid the full price so He can give you all He has as a free gift. If something is a gift, then how can you possibly earn it? You can only receive it with gratitude. If you will learn to do this with God, then you will truly be understanding the heart of the Gospel of Jesus Christ.

Let's go to the first of these other two references in the New Testament which quote the verse, *"Abraham believed God, and it was reckoned to him as righteousness."*

ROMANS 4:1-3

In the fourth chapter of Paul's letter to the Church at Rome, he was in the midst of a discussion on the topic of justification. The Greek word Paul used for justification in this text was, "dik-ah-yo'-o", which means: to show as just, innocent, free; to justify, and make righteous. Paul stated that this is what occurs when we place our faith in Christ for salvation. We become justified. Even though we were dead in our trespasses, God makes us innocent and free. He makes us righteous. As Paul wrote in another place, *"By His doing you are in Christ Jesus, Who became to us wisdom from God, and righteousness and sanctification, and redemption"* (1st Corinthians 1:30).

The particular passage of Scripture I want to dwell upon says, *"What then shall we say that Abraham, our forefather according to the flesh, has found? For if Abraham was justified by works, he has something to boast about; but not before God. For what does the Scripture say? 'And Abraham believed God, and it was reckoned to him as righteousness'"* (Romans 4:1-3).

According to this Scripture, how was Abraham justified? How did he become just, innocent and free? Was it through his own works, efforts, and accomplishments? No, it was by faith, by belief. What was it Abraham believed? In this context, as Paul teaches, Abraham believed that God would justify him instead of he having to justify himself.

If we are going to get anywhere at all in our friendship with God, we must first have a firm understanding of our salvation in Christ. Salvation is not something we earn. It is a gift. God earned salvation for us. Would you ever think of saying to God, "Look, God, I realize Jesus died for my sins, but I just don't think

33

that's enough, so I'm going to try to earn my salvation?" You would never say that to God, would you? Yet, many people do live in that type of understanding about God. By not realizing the salvation which is theirs as a free gift in Jesus Christ, they plod along, hoping to arrive some day at the point where their good works will be enough to earn them salvation. It will never happen that way, simply because you cannot earn something that has already been given to you as a free gift.

In Paul's letter to the church of the Ephesians he made this point just about as clear as anyone could make it when he wrote, *"For by grace you have been saved through faith; and that not of yourselves, it is the gift of God; not as a result of works, that no one should boast" (2:8-9).* God's grace saves you. Grace is God paying for your sins when you could not. *"For you know the grace of our Lord Jesus Christ, that though He was rich, yet for your sake He became poor, so that you through His poverty might become rich" (2nd Corinthians 8:9).* Grace is Jesus dying on the cross at Calvary, taking your place. Grace is God offering you life with Him without requiring you to work for it. Grace is your being made a new creation in Jesus Christ out of God's love for you. *"By grace you have been saved."* Grace is 100% God and 0% you. God's grace has done it all. All that is left for you to do is to receive

His grace.

Through your faith and reception, God's grace becomes activated and vibrantly alive in your own life. It's by grace you are saved, and not by works. Works are what you do whereas grace is what God does.

So, the first thing we must understand, in our friendship with God, is the nature of our salvation. If we will see that it is totally a gift from God to us, and if we are willing to receive salvation as a gift, then we will have a clear road and ability to grow in our friendship with God. How was Abraham justified? Simply by believing. Because he believed God would justify him, justification became real to him.

GALATIANS 3:5-6

Here is the other place in the New Testament where Abraham's justification by faith is referred to. This time Paul quoted the verse from Genesis in a completely different context from the one in Romans. Paul wrote, *"Does He then who provides you with the Spirit and works miracles among you, do it by the works of the Law, or by hearing with faith? Even so 'Abraham believed God, and it was reckoned to him as righteousness'"* (Galatians 3:5-6).

I think this must have been one of Paul's favorite verses. It seems he thought about it a lot. In talking about the nature of our salvation, he quotes it. And in this place, talking about our ongoing walk in the Lord, he quotes it again.

Think about Paul's own life for a moment and you will see why this verse meant so much to him.

Paul wasn't always a Christian. The Book of Acts tells us that before he was converted, Paul hated Christians. He hated Christians so much that he would hunt them down and arrest them. Once, he even held the coats of his fellows while they stoned a Christian to death *(Acts 7:58 - 8:3)*. But when God confronted Paul, on his way to Damascus, he became a changed man *(Acts 9)*. Paul realized he had actually been fighting against God, while all that time he thought he had been fighting for God. In relating his former manner of life Paul said, *"I thought to myself that I had to do many things hostile to the name of Jesus of Nazareth. And this is just what I did in Jerusalem; not only did I lock up many of the saints in prisons, having received authority from the chief priests, but also when they were being put to death I cast my vote against them. And as I punished them often in all the synagogues, I tried to force them to blaspheme; and being furiously enraged at them, I kept pursuing them even to foreign cities" (Acts 26: 9-11)*. Paul had thought he was doing God a big favor by trying to wipe out the Christians. However, when Paul became converted in the dust of that Damascus road, he saw how deceptive and filthy his own self-righteousness was.

Paul came to the painful realization that he had actually been killing God's own children. And yet, God loved him anyway. Now that's grace!

I can see why this verse about Abraham meant so much to Paul. I'm sure Paul felt he deserved to die for all he had done against the Lord. But God justified Paul, and Paul clung to that grace throughout the rest of his life. Having come out of a background of thinking spirituality was produced by obedience to the Law, Paul knew how dangerous trusting in works was.

So, once again, Paul used this verse. However, this time he was dealing with a different subject than justification. Here is the question he asked the Galatians, *"Does He then who provides you with the Spirit and works miracles among you, do it by works of the Law, or by hearing with faith?"* In other words, is your receiving the Spirit and the miracle power of God a question of what you do or is it a question of what God does? Do you earn God's anointing, power and blessings through the works of the Law, or does God give these things to you as a gift of grace, just as He gives salvation and justification? And then, to answer his own question, Paul quoted this familiar text from Genesis, *"Abraham believed God, and it was reckoned to him as righteousness."*

Receiving the Spirit is a matter of believing in God's grace, just in the same way you believe for salvation. Receiving the miracles of God is a matter of believing by faith, just like you believe for your justification. It is not by works; it is by grace.

It is significant that Paul used the same Scripture in speaking about salvation and about growth. In essence, he was saying that our entire life of faith is a never ending response to the magnificent grace of God. We are saved by grace and we grow by grace. We begin by grace and we continue in grace.

In his letter to the church of the Colossians, Paul wrote, *"As you therefore received Christ Jesus the Lord, so walk in Him,"(2:6)*. This means you are saved by grace, and you are kept by grace.

God is not in the business of changing horses in midstream. Unfortunately, many Christians are under the impression that this is exactly what God does. They are told, on the one hand, they cannot earn their salvation, and that's right. We have seen this fact. There is no way you could possibly earn your salvation, no way at all. So, these people gladly receive Jesus as Savior through faith, and they become justified. They are made righteous, free, and innocent - so far so good.

But what happens next, in many cases, is not good at all. After receiving the grace of God for salvation, many Christians are then told it is completely up to them to keep themselves saved. God has, in effect, changed horses in midstream. He used one method to get you saved and now, according to some, he has a different method to keep you saved. His grace gave you the greatest gift of all time: new life in Jesus Christ. But somehow, in this mistaken understanding, God's grace isn't big enough to give you the rest of what He has for you. Does that make sense? No, not at all. The Bible clearly states that in the same way we received Christ as Savior, by grace, so should we walk in Him, again, by grace.

By using the example of Abraham in both settings, that of salvation and in growth, Paul was making it abundantly clear that all we have, or ever will have, comes totally as a free gift by the grace of God. God doesn't ask us to earn these blessings. All God asks is that we would be willing to receive what He has for us by faith.

If we are to understand our friendship with God, we must first understand our salvation. It is by grace and not works, lest anyone should boast. And concerning our walk in the Lord, we must understand it is once again by grace and not by works that we are given the Holy

Spirit and the miracle working power of God in our life. As we see and become gratefully aware of these truths, we will have the foundation laid for a strong relationship with the Lord. By trusting in His strength, and not your own, you will never be let down.

Suppose you went to your next door neighbor's house and asked to borrow their lawn mower. You ask politely only to hear the reply, "I can't give it to you because you already have it. I gave it to you last week." Would you then respond by saying, "Look, I'll give you ten dollars if only you will let me borrow your lawn mower"? If you did say that, your neighbor would think you were crazy. You know you wouldn't say that. If you already had it, you wouldn't need to ask for it and if you already had it, you wouldn't need to do anything to get it.

This is what God's Word is saying. You can't earn anything from God because He has already earned everything for you. In the same way that it would be ridiculous for you to ask your neighbor to lend you something you already had, it would also be ridiculous for you to try to earn what God has already paid for and graciously given you.

You have probably heard the expression, "Believing is receiving." Well, in the context of what Paul is teaching in Galatians and Romans, believing *is* receiving. By faith in God's work, you are justified; and by faith in God's work, you have His Spirit and power.

Understanding this, let's now go to the original place where this phrase, *"Abraham believed God, and it was reckoned to him as righteousness"* first appears.

GENESIS 15

Abraham wanted a son. He wanted an heir who would carry on his name and heritage. However, Abraham and his wife, Sarah, had been married many years and they had been unable to have any children.

In the first verse of Genesis 15, we are told, *"The word of the Lord came to Abram in a vision, saying, 'Do not fear, Abram, I am a shield to you; your reward shall be very great.'"*

Those are good words, aren't they? The Lord was saying, figuratively, that we don't have to have any fear because He is our shield. God often presents Himself to us in illustrative ways, such as being a shield, so that we may be able to more fully understand and appreciate all He is to us. If we were to ignore God's word we might have fear, for we would not be aware of His protection. But He comes to us and is delighted to tell us He is our shield.

What was Abraham's reaction to these words? Did he fall on the ground and praise

God? No, not exactly. Abraham replied, *"O Lord God, what will you give me, since I am childless?" (Genesis 15:2)*. At this point, Abraham was more concerned with his own problems than with God's promises. God's words could not penetrate Abraham's heart because he was caught up with his own affairs.

Abraham wasn't able to appreciate God's promise. He wanted a son. It's just as if God had come to Abraham and said He was going to bless him, and Abraham replied, "Well, that's nice God, but what about my problem here?" Abraham was being problem-conscious, or self-conscious, rather than being God-conscious. God was actually trying to get through to Abraham about his problem, but Abraham wasn't in the right frame of mind, at that moment, to receive God's word.

Isn't it odd how we also do this? We may find ourselves in a particular need, and we may go to God in prayer about it, asking Him to meet the need. And yet, when God does come to us with an encouraging word, many times we shut Him off because we don't see how it relates to our problem. This doesn't sound rational, but it happens all the time. It's like going to the doctor and telling him what your illness is, but refusing to take the medicine he prescribes. When we let ourselves slip into a problem-conscious state rather than a Christ-

conscious state, we are actually locking ourselves into the very problem we need an
answer to. When we bring a matter to the Lord
in prayer, we need to give it to Him, and leave
it with Him. Then, after having prayed, we
need to take our mind off the difficulty and
place it upon Christ, for He is the answer to
our need. This is what the apostle Peter meant
when he wrote, *"Casting all your anxiety upon
Him, because He cares for you"* (1st Peter 5:7).

At this point though, Abraham still needed
to learn that lesson. His response to God's
Word was, *"O Lord God, what wilt Thou give me,
since I am childless, and the heir of my house is
Eliezer of Damascus?"* It's as if Abraham was
saying, "Listen God, as long as I don't have a
son, I'm afraid nothing you can give me will be
all that thrilling." Abraham didn't understand
that God was talking about giving him a son.

Abraham knew he and Sarah were not able
to produce a child by their own strength, so he
tried to figure out a solution using his own
intellect. He said, "God, I don't have a son, so
let's take Eliezer and we can pretend he's my
child." Abraham was still trusting in his own
resources, rather than trusting in the word of
the Lord. Well, God wasn't about to go for
that one. Abraham went on to say, in verse
three, *"Since Thou hast given no offspring to me,
one born in my house is my heir."* Abraham was

43

essentially making God his scapegoat. "It's all your fault, God. You haven't given me a son. You're the cause of all my misery." It's pretty clear that at this point, God and Abraham weren't exactly sharing an intimate friendship.

But look at what God did. *"Then behold, the word of the Lord came to him saying, 'This man will not be your heir; but one who shall come forth from your own body, he shall be your heir.' And He took him outside and said, 'Now look toward the heavens, and count the stars, if you are able to count them.' And He said to him, 'So shall your descendants be.'"*

God's love for Abraham was not about to be turned aside by Abraham's negative attitude. God wanted to give Abraham the desire of his heart, so He showed him the stars and told him his descendants would be that numerous. Abraham had tried to produce a child through his own efforts and he had failed. Now he was trying to get God to agree with him that Eliezer would be his heir. He was still trying to do things his own way, according to his own rationality. But God responded by giving him a promise that was far greater than anything he had ever dreamed. God was saying, "Abraham, stop trying so hard. Relax. We don't need Eliezer, because I'm going to bring my promise to pass right through you."

Abraham could have said, "No God, I'll

keep trying. I'll keep working at it. I'll keep try-ing to earn the blessing you want to give me." But Abraham didn't say that. Or, Abraham could have responded with the "I'm not worthy" attitude. But he didn't.

At last the light was turned on in Abraham's heart. For once he stopped looking at his own problems and abilities, or lack of abilities in this case, and he started looking at what God was saying. Verse 6 says, *"Then he believed in the Lord; and He reckoned it to him as righteousness."* At the moment Abraham took his eyes up off of himself and placed them upon God, he was made righteous. And as James 2:23 says, *"'Abraham believed God, and it was reckoned to him as righteousness,' and he was called the friend of God."*

How was Abraham made righteous? By choosing to believe God would accomplish His purpose in him, apart from his help. At that point, Abraham understood that God would bring forth His promise in him totally by His Own will and power. There was nothing more that Abraham could do. He was helpless and he finally realized what God had been trying to get across to him all along. God had never said to Abraham that the two of them would bring forth a son. It was never a you-plus-Me proposition. God had made an unconditional statement that He would bless Abraham, period. It wasn't until Abraham had run out of his own resources that he was willing to believe. But Abraham finally did believe. He at last received the grace of God, and God made him righteous and His friend.

Do you see from all this how you become God's friend? Are you willing to believe like Abraham? Perhaps you have thought it is up to you to earn a good standing, or keep a good standing, with God. Maybe you've thought you have to struggle to gain God's promise and approval. Please, will you receive this friendship as a gift? This is the only way you will be able to realize Christ as your friend. And this is the only way you will be able to grow in your friendship with God. This is God's way and it's wonderful. As we have seen, it's by grace you are saved. It's by grace you receive the Spirit and miracles, and it's by grace you receive your friendship with God.

You become God's friend by believing He wants to be your Friend. It's that simple. But the simplicity of it is the very stumbling block for so many. There always seems to be the thought lurking around in the back of one's mind about what one must do.

Let me tell you something about the grace of God. Romans 11:6 says, *"But if it is by grace, it is no longer on the basis of works, otherwise grace is no longer grace."* If God gives you something by His grace then, according to this verse, it would be impossible for you to play any part in earning it. Otherwise grace could not be grace. Grace, by its very definition here, <u>has</u> to stand alone. Don't let anyone ever present a mixture of grace and works to you. Actually, all they would be giving you, in reality, is works. Your friendship with God is a gift from God. How sad it is that there are so many who refuse to receive this truly marvelous gift. I trust you will give God the joy of His heart by gratefully accepting His glorious gift.

<u>A FRIENDSHIP</u>
<u>COVENANT OF GRACE</u>

Let me give you another example of God's grace in friendship. After Abraham decided to place his faith in God and not in himself, the Lord told Abraham to prepare to cut a covenant. This was a cultural practice in those days. When two parties wanted to come to a binding agreement on a matter, they would take sacrificial animals, cut them in half, and lay them out in two rows, the halves facing each other. When that was completed, the two parties involved would walk between the pieces. This would publicly make their agreement binding. By walking through these animal pieces together they were, in effect, saying, "May what has been done to these animals be done to us if we should ever break our covenant."

When God told Abraham to prepare the animals, Abraham knew God was referring to cutting a covenant. What Abraham didn't know was that God was going to use this ceremony in order to teach him even more about His grace and promises. After Abraham prepared the animals, Scripture says, *"Now when the sun was going down, a deep sleep fell upon Abram." (Genesis 15:12).* God caused Abraham to fall asleep, and it was while Abraham was asleep that God made His oaths, or agreements. Abraham could not make an oath in return, because he was asleep. Verse 17 goes on to say, *"And it came about that when the sun had set, that it was very dark, and behold, there appeared a smoking oven and a flaming torch which passed between these pieces. On that day the Lord made a covenant with Abram."*

God made the covenant, not Abraham. God made the promises, not Abraham. God took all the responsibilities, not Abraham. Through causing Abraham to fall asleep, so he couldn't walk through the pieces, God was showing His friend that this was a covenant of grace. This was a covenant based totally upon what God promised to do, and had nothing at all to do with Abraham making any vows in return.

Receive your friendship with God in this

way. If you do want to say something to God in return, just tell Him you are forever grateful and intend to enjoy your friendship with Him to the fullest extent.

In closing this chapter, let me share with you a verse of Scripture from Proverbs -*"He who values grace and truth is the King's friend"* *(Proverbs 22:11, Living Bible).* You see, it is the one who drinks in the grace and truth of God who is able to truly appreciate and understand his, or her, friendship with the Lord. Look at grace and you will be seeing Jesus. Look at truth and you will see Jesus. Value the grace and truth God has freely given you through Jesus Christ and you will be drawn into your friendship with God.

You are the King's Friend! I hope it is abundantly clear to you that this relationship of being friends with God is simply a matter of your willingness to accept what He has said and done on your behalf. God's Word is beautifully clear and to the point. *"Abraham believed God, and it was reckoned to him as righteousness,' and he was called the friend of God."* I encourage you to insert your own name in this verse. Believe God and have it reckoned to you as righteousness. Do this and you will know yourself as "the friend of God."

CHAPTER 3

HEARING
YOUR FRIEND

If there is one voice you can look forward to hearing, it's the voice of your Friend.

In this chapter I would like to take a look at the relationship between being a friend with God and being able to hear His voice. As I have studied Scripture about our friendship with God I have been surprised by the amount of verses that tie these two subjects together. I have discovered that developing our friendship with God puts us in a position to more clearly and closely hear His voice. In some of the Scriptures I'm going to share with you, we will see that these two subjects are actually inseparable.

Do you want to hear God's voice? Do you think this is important, or do you think you can manage without it? I hope you do want to hear His voice, for Jesus said, in the 10th chapter of the Gospel of John, *"My sheep hear My voice" (verse 27)*. What does this mean? In what way can you hear His voice? If you are not seeing God as your friend, then chances are you will have a very difficult time hearing His voice.

You have an image of God. Somewhere inside of you there is a mental concept of what God is like. If He is not your friend, then He must be something else to you. Perhaps you view Him as the hard taskmaster who is just waiting to let you have it the first time you slip up. Obviously, if that's your picture of God, you won't be eager to hear from Him. Or maybe you see Him as your Savior, but as a rather disinterested Savior Who really doesn't care that much about you in a personal way. Once again, if that's your concept of God, you will probably have difficulty hearing His voice because you will not believe He would take the time to talk to you in the first place. The basic point I'm making is this; if there isn't a healthy relationship and understanding between you and God, then communication is going to be a problem.

But think of this for a moment. What a joy it is for you to talk with your best friend. You're always glad to hear that voice because you know love, acceptance, and genuine affection will be expressed to you. You don't have to worry about being put down or criticized.

It's good to hear your best friend's voice, isn't it? Think now of the possibilities in your life if you will allow God to be your Best Friend, and if you will accept the fact that He thinks of you as His friend.

Can you see that how you look at God determines the type of communication you will have with Him? In developing your friendship with God, hearing His voice will become the delight of your heart.

Back now to John 10:27, *"My sheep hear My voice."* How could you, as one of His sheep, hear His voice? I believe the answer is found in the Book of Hebrews. Three times in the space of two chapters, the author of this epistle quotes the same Scripture. Originally from the ninety-fifth Psalm, the text says, *"Today if ye will hear His voice, harden not your hearts" (Hebrews 3:7&15, 4:7 King James).* If you truly want to hear God's voice, you must first believe you <u>can</u> hear His voice. If you refuse to believe this, then you would be, essentially, "hardening your heart."

In this section of Hebrews, Chapters 3 and 4, the author was speaking about entering into the rest of the Lord. Using the nation of Israel as an example, he wrote about what happens when God's people refuse to believe Him. In Israel's case, they refused to believe God had given them the promised land. So they said, "We're not going in there." God's reply was, "all right, you won't go in. As a matter of fact, you will never enter." And that ushered in 40 years of wandering in the wilderness. God would not let His people into their land of rest until that generation of unbelief had perished. Hebrews 3:19 says, *"And so we see that they were not able to enter because of unbelief."* This example shows us that God can be restricted from bringing His will to pass in our lives if we have unbelieving hearts. An unbelieving heart is a hardened heart.

The writer of Hebrews goes on to say to Christians that we should not be like Israel. If we refuse to believe God's Word, we too may be keeping ourselves from realizing God's promises in our own lives. Speaking on the subject of rest, Chapter 4, verse 3 says, *"For we who have believed enter that rest."* What is it that we are to believe? The answer is found in the 10th verse of Chapter 4; *"For the one who has entered His rest has himself also rested from his works."* In order to experience the rest God offers us, we must stop struggling, trying to earn rest, and instead must believe that God has already secured rest for us. By exhibiting unbelief, we would in effect be saying, "God hasn't done this for me. I must do it on my own." It is when we are willing to cease from our works (trying mistakenly to earn His favor when He has already favored us) that we are able to experientially enter the rest Christ has for us.

We need to stop working long enough to see what God has done. I can easily say that many of the things we strive so hard to attain have, in fact, already been provided for us by Jesus Christ. If we will be still and know He is God *(Psalm 46:10)*, then we will stop working so hard, and fruitlessly, and will instead be praising God for all He has done.

This is what I am saying regarding your friendship with God. Refusing to believe what I am sharing with you from Scripture will be like a self-fulfilling prophecy. If you say, "It can't be true. I'm not God's friend, not little old me. Only a special group of Christians who are stronger than I can be God's friend." Then, sure enough, if that's your frame of mind, you probably never will realize Christ as your friend. Unbelief will harden your heart, and you won't be able to hear God's voice.

This brings us full circle back to the question of hearing God's voice. Most obviously, you can hear God speak to you as you read Scripture. These are His words to you. He is speaking to you.

Take, for example, the Scripture from John 15 that we looked at in the first chapter. I showed you what the Word said. Jesus said it. It's true. But, if you deflect the truth I've shared with you by saying it can't be for you, then you would not be allowing God to speak to you through this Word. However, by receiving those words as being for you, you would be allowing God to speak to you. And it would no longer be an impersonal Scripture. It would become the Bread of Life. The Word would feed you and bless you, giving you direction and confidence in your relationship with God.

How can you hear God's voice? By accepting the truth of Scripture in a personal way. Unfortunately, many Christians have gotten into the habit of reading the Bible much like they would read any other book. The words are there, but they remain distant and impersonal. They're not allowing the Word to become flesh. It's only when you believe God's Word in a personal way that you are letting yourself hear His voice.

It is crucial for you to hear God's voice. Back in the 10th chapter of the Gospel of John, Jesus said, referring to Himself as our Good Shepherd, *"The sheep follow him because they know his voice" (verse 4)*. The point Jesus made here is that our ability to follow Him depends upon our knowing His voice. Without that we won't know how to follow Him.

And in the 3rd verse of the same chapter, He said, *"The sheep hear his voice, and he calls his own sheep by name, and leads them out."* Two important truths are expressed here. The first is that

Jesus, our Good Shepherd, calls His own sheep by name. Now, that's personal. Do you know and accept that our Savior calls you by name? You mean something to Him. He knows you and looks upon you as an individual; an individual friend. A one-to-one relationship is what is being spoken of in this verse. The second point is the phrase, *"he leads them out."* By being willing to hear God's voice, you will be giving Jesus an opportunity to lead you.

Do you want to be led of the Lord? Do you want to be able to follow Him? Do you want to have a personal relationship with Him? These Scriptures say you can have all this just by hearing His voice. And, once again, you can hear His voice simply by believing what His Word says. I'm speaking of belief in a personal way, not belief in a merely historical way, accepting the fact that Jesus did at one time say this. *"Today if ye will hear His voice, harden not your hearts."* By receiving the truth of God's Word as being for yourself, personally, you will be hearing God's voice.

MOSES: AN EXAMPLE OF COMMUNICATION IN FRIENDSHIP

In looking at the relationship between being a friend of God and being able to hear His voice, I think the example of Moses is a great place to start.

Who can doubt Moses heard the Lord's voice? This is the man God used to bring His people out of 400 years of bondage in Egypt. Moses may have been reluctant to hear God's voice at first, but he definitely did hear it and he came to know God in an intimate way. Moses was clearly led by God and he was able to follow because he heard God's voice.

Think about this verse, *"Thus the Lord used to speak to Moses face to face, just as a man speaks to his friend" (Exodus 33:11).*

This was the type of communication God established with Moses, *"face to face, just as a man speaks to his friend."* Moses was more than a slave. He was more than just a tool in the hand of God. He was a friend, and God spoke to him as a friend.

This is the type of communication God desires to establish with you; a complete and total honesty, a baring of souls to each other, so to speak, a face-to-face communication, just as a man speaks to his friend.

Have you ever noticed if you are talking with someone whom you don't particularly like, that you very seldom look them in the eye? Or have you ever noticed when someone confronts you with a criticism, or some other bad news, that there is very little face-to-face contact? You may look at your hands, the floor, the ceiling, or anywhere but the other person's face. Looking someone in the face is a sign of confidence and of a strong relationship. You don't feel nervous or threatened. You can look them in the face.

That's the way it was with God and Moses. They spoke face to face. God looked Moses in the face, and Moses looked God in the face, in the sense that they shared an intimate friendship with each other.

Let me give you an idea of the things God used to say to Moses in this face-to-face friendship. In verse 13 of Exodus 33, Moses said to God, *"Now therefore, I pray Thee, if I have found favor in Thy sight, let me know Thy ways, that I may know Thee, so that I may find favor in Thy sight."* Do you see the circle in this verse? Moses' words begin and end with the topic of finding favor in God's sight. I think it's implied here that Moses knew he had found favor in God's sight. He knew he was pleasing to God. That's a hallmark of real friendship, realizing you are pleasing to the sight of your friend. So Moses said, "Show me your ways." In other words, He was saying, "reveal even more of yourself to me God." Why did Moses want to know more about God? *"That I may know Thee."* He knew the more he got to know about God, the better he would actually know God in a personal way. And, as he grew in the knowledge of God, he knew he would always find favor in God's sight. This is not speaking of a service-oriented relationship, but of a relationship based upon love.

If you will understand that you are pleasing to God, you will have a growing desire to know His ways. You will want to know more of the true nature of the Lord Who loves you so. And, as you discover an increasing knowledge of God, you will be even further fortified in the fact that you are pleasing in His sight.

What was God's reply to Moses' request? Verse 14 says, *"And He said, 'My presence shall go with you, and I will give you rest.'"*

If God said this to you today, you would be jumping up and down for joy, wouldn't you? So let me tell you something. God does want to say this to you today. He wants to take this Scripture right up off the page and plant it in your own heart. These are the types of things you'll be able to hear God speaking to you as you grow in a communication with Him based upon friendship. You'll know you have the continuous presence of God in your life. We saw previously that His word says, *"I will never leave you nor forsake you"* (Hebrews 13:5). As friends, you will readily believe this truth in your own life because you will be growing in the understanding of God's true nature.

"I will give you rest." We have seen this

earlier in this chapter. You can relax in His love and be at ease as you serve Him, because you are His friend.

MOUTH TO MOUTH
COMMUNICATION

Another portion of Scripture about Moses' friendship and communication with God is found in the book of Numbers. At this particular time, Moses' own brother and sister had turned against him. They had been through some rough times and had decided to make Moses their scapegoat. The beautiful thing here, though, is that before Moses even got a chance to answer his family's criticism, God Himself answered them. God ran to Moses' defense and took care of Aaron and Miriam *(Numbers 12:1-16)*.

What about you? Will you believe God loves you to the extent that He will take care of your trials and adversaries? Before you would even have a chance to compose yourself enough to fight back, God would already have the situation under control. Now that's friendship, isn't it?

I would like to give special attention to something God said to Miriam and Aaron when He was standing up for Moses. In Numbers, Chapter 12 verse 8, this is what the Lord said about His friend, Moses: *"With him I speak mouth to mouth, even openly, and not in dark sayings, and he beholds the form of the Lord."*

We saw earlier that God spoke with Moses face to face. Here we encounter a different term, *"mouth to mouth."* Face to face speaks of a direct communication, while I believe mouth to mouth is purposely used here to speak of a close communication.

You've heard of mouth-to-mouth resuscitation, where the breath of one person gives breath and life to another. Well, think of mouth-to-mouth communication as the words of God giving breath and life to your innermost being.

You certainly can't get any closer to someone than mouth to mouth. I believe God was saying here, "Moses and I are as close as two can get." Isn't that great? I think that's fantastic. I am absolutely thrilled to think that as I grow with God, we will get as close as two can get.

It's an unspoken rule of conversation, in our culture, that when you speak with someone, you stand about 18 inches away from them. Everybody feels comfortable with that. Get any closer and you may threaten or make uncomfortable the one with whom you are talking. Speaking mouth to mouth is something we would think only lovers do. In our society, that's the way it is. What I'm getting at is that this is how close God desires to be with you;

mouth to mouth close.

<u>OPEN</u>
<u>COMMUNICATION</u>

God went on to say He spoke with Moses, *"even openly, and not in dark sayings."* Do you ever get the feeling God's words are like dark sayings? You may see them, but you don't know what they mean. I think I can explain this verse best by referring to something Jesus said.

In the 13th chapter of the Gospel of Matthew, Jesus taught the multitudes the Parable of the Sower. Afterwards, Scripture says the disciples came to Jesus and said, *"Why do You speak to them in parables?"* In other words, why do you speak in dark sayings? Why not make it clear and simple?

Jesus replied, *"I speak to them in parables because while seeing they do not see, and while hearing they do not hear, nor do they understand"* *(Matthew 13:13).* And then He said to the disciples, *"But blessed are your eyes, because they see; and your ears because they hear"* *(verse 16).*

Here's the question. What was the difference between the multitudes and the disciples? Why did some see while others didn't? The answer is actually quite simple.

Jesus taught the multitudes the parable of the sower, but it was only the disciples who came to Him for the explanation. The others just went their own way. Jesus' sayings remained dark sayings for them because they didn't take the time to ask Him what He meant. However, the disciples went right to Jesus and said, "What are you saying?" If you go on in Matthew 13, you will see Jesus went through the parable again, and made it easy for the disciples to understand.

Those with the closer relationship were able to see and hear, while those who were more distant had ears, but didn't hear; and had eyes, but didn't see. Perhaps there were some in that multitude who thought, as they walked away, "I'd like to ask Jesus what that meant, but He doesn't have time for me." If only they knew, right? Meanwhile, the disciples thought, "I'm going to ask Jesus to explain this to me."

What's the moral of this portion of Scripture? The closer your relationship with God is, the clearer your understanding of Him will be and the more confidence you will possess in seeking Him.

So, when God said He spoke with Moses, *"even openly, and not in dark sayings,"* He was saying, "Moses and I are close. I explain all My words and plans to Him."

You can be that close with God. As a matter of fact, I believe this is precisely His will for you.

Don't shortchange yourself! Don't keep

God's words in the realm of dark sayings. If there is something you don't understand, go to Him with it. Ask Him to make it clear to you. God may be purposely putting dark sayings in front of you, not to confuse you or make you feel distant, but so you will come to Him and let Him make them clear to you, just like He did for His disciples in the case of the parable of the sower.

BEHOLDING
THE FORM OF THE LORD

This brings us to the third statement God made in this Scripture from Numbers about Moses, *"And He beholds the form of the Lord"* (12:8).

You won't be able to see this third truth in your own life unless you are willing to accept the first two truths. First comes the knowledge of a mouth-to-mouth communication. This leads to speaking openly and not in dark sayings. And that will bring you to the place where you will be able to behold the form of the Lord.

What does it mean to behold the form of the Lord? It means you can see what God is like. It means you can see Him at all times. You behold the form of the Lord.

Let God speak mouth to mouth with you today. Let Him speak openly, and not in dark sayings. Do this, and His form will begin to

65

appear. God won't be hidden away in the fog. He'll be clear to you, and you'll know His presence with you.

Moses was God's friend. God was Moses' Friend. Because of this, Moses knew God's presence was always with him. He experienced rest. He spoke with God face to face and mouth to mouth. He understood things clearly, and he beheld the form of the Lord. All of these things Moses realized from hearing God's voice, and he heard God's voice because he and God were friends.

ABOUT
SEEKING SIGNS

I'd like to draw aside for a moment and ask you to think about something. As we've looked at Moses, I hope you are seeing the blessing of possessing a close communication with God, and I hope you are looking forward to your own growth in this area of your life with God. However, in studying this, God has brought something to my mind, and it has to do with asking Him for signs.

Have you ever had the experience of witnessing to somebody about Jesus Christ, only to hear this type of response, "I'll believe God is real if He shakes the earth under my feet right now" or, "I'll believe in God if He writes my name in the sky or sends me a personal telegram?" Sounds silly, doesn't it? What would you say to someone who responded to the Gospel like that? I know I'd say, "God's message came to you loud and clear at the cross of Calvary. God's personal invitation to you is expressed through the death and resurrection of Jesus Christ. If you will receive Him as your own Savior and Lord, believing He died for your sins, then you will be born again."

How is it that God communicates His plan of salvation? Is it by granting the unusual requests and demands such as I've listed above? No. God's way of communication is well expressed in the first chapter of Hebrews; *"In these last days [He] has spoken to us in His Son" (1:2).* God's message is complete. True faith is accepting God's Word, not disregarding God's Word by demanding some special sign.

I'd like you to think about this now in regard to your own relationship with the Lord. Sometimes we ask God for a sign. We may be in some troubling situation and we might say, "Oh God, I need a sign from you." Do you realize it's possible that our asking God for a sign could be a sign to us of laziness on our part? Our request for a sign may really be us saying, "God, I don't want to take the time to develop a communication based upon friendship with You, so just show me a sign."

It's easy to offer a quick prayer and say,

"Show me a sign." It's a little harder to take the time to go into God's Word, study the Scriptures, pray about a matter and wait upon the Lord for a word from Him. It takes a commitment to dialogue with God. It can be a cop-out to say, "Show me a sign."

Not only that, but the show-me-a-sign mentality can actually rob you of precious times of communication you could be experiencing with God on a daily basis. I would much prefer to have God personally communicate with me and direct me by His Spirit than to simply show me a sign. Don't get me wrong. God does give us signs. I know He does. But something is wrong if His children are always asking for signs.

When I was young in the Lord, I'm afraid I related to God more through a sign-seeking way rather than through communication with Him via His Word. For instance, if I needed an answer to something, I'd play spiritual darts with the Bible. You know, close your eyes, flip open the Bible, and poke at a verse. God actually did, on occasion, give direction to me in that way. What else could He do? I was a baby, and He spoke to me like one. But a mature Christian ought to know better. If you need an answer, you study Scripture. You don't play games with it. You pray about it. You don't demand instant results. You wait upon the

Lord. You don't impatiently jump to conclusions. See what I mean? Our interest in signs could actually be a sign of a rather shallow or undeveloped relationship with the Lord. If one is not willing to take the time to establish a good, solid friendship with God, one may never get beyond the sign-seeking stage.

If a friendship is to be successful, it will take time and commitment. I've shown you in this chapter that God is committed to you and is willing to take the time with you. What will your response be? Are you committed and willing to take the time? The decision is up to you. You can go on relating to God in a "give-me-a-sign" way, essentially keeping Him at a distance. Or you can joyously enter into the face-to-face and mouth-to-mouth communication God desires to have with you, experiencing the joys of daily communion with your Creator and Best Friend.

CHAPTER 4

THE BLESSINGS OF HEARING YOUR FRIEND

Embracing your friendship with God enables you to hear His voice.

I want to share with you four distinct blessings that are yours. You will be able to know these four blessings only as you allow God to be your Friend. If you will do that, then the avenue will be open for you to hear His voice, and these four truths from Scripture will become glorious reality in your life.

THE BLESSING OF DESIRE

For the first blessing, let me share two Scriptures with you, both from the Song of Solomon. The first is found in Chapter 5, verse 16; *"His mouth is full of sweetness. And He is wholly desirable. This is my beloved and this is my friend."*

71

There are two main characters in the Song of Solomon, the bride and the bridegroom. These particular words are spoken by the bride. This book is an allegory of the desired relationship between Christ and the believer. The bridegroom represents Christ and the bride represents you, the believer. So, in this particular verse it is the bride, or believer, speaking of the bridegroom, or Christ.

Allow this verse to sink in for a moment. *"His mouth is full of sweetness. And He is wholly desirable. This is my beloved and this is my friend."* Let these words minister to you.

The first blessing is: through your friendship <u>with</u> God you will have a growing desire <u>for</u> God. *"He is wholly desirable."*

There are two reasons given in this verse as to why the bridegroom is wholly desirable. The first is, *"His mouth is full of sweetness."*

Do you know that God's words are sweet? Are they sweet to you?

I have counseled with people who are actually afraid to read the Bible because every time they open it, they feel condemned. They may take some verse out of context and, due to an extremely poor understanding of God, they condemn themselves with it. Instead of knowing the sweetness of God's Word, it is bitter to them.

Psalm 19, verse 10 says this concerning

God's words, *"They are more desirable than gold, yes, than much fine gold; sweeter also than honey and the drippings of the honeycomb."*

God's words are sweet. They are life. They are spiritual food. If you know the sweetness of God's words, you will find yourself desiring Him more and more.

The second reason why you'll desire God, and I might add it's also the reason why you can know the sweetness of His words, is found in the latter part of this verse from the Song of Solomon. *"This is my beloved and this is my friend."* Again we are brought to friendship with God. And this is an intimate friendship. God isn't just called friend here. He is also called beloved. Put the two together and you have "beloved friend." That's the kind of Friend God is, or wants to be, to you, a Beloved Friend, a Friend Whom you love.

Knowing the sweetness of His voice, and knowing Him as a Beloved Friend, adds up to your having a growing desire for God. *"He is wholly desirable."* As you personally hear His words of encouragement to you, the natural outcome will be a desire for more of Him. Isn't it much better to desire God out of genuine affection, rather than out of a sense of spiritual obligation and duty? Of course it is, and this is exactly what God has for you, as you hear the sweet words of your Friend.

The second Scripture concerning a growing desire for God is found in the eighth chapter of the Song Of Solomon. Verse 13 says, *"O you who sit in the gardens, my companions are listening for your voice - let me hear it!"* What does the phrase, *"O you who sit in the gardens,"* make you think of? It makes me think of quiet, peaceful, and serene surroundings.

It's pretty hard to imagine God sitting quietly in a garden condemning you. It would seem out of character. I can only imagine words of comfort and love being spoken in a setting such as this. And this is why the verse says, *"Let me hear it!"* If you knew God had a good word waiting for you, you would want to hear it, wouldn't you? Well, God does have good words for you and your knowledge of this will give you the desire for more and more of Him.

As Christians, we are exhorted to grow. Growth is to be the path of life for us spiritually, just as it is for us physically. Wouldn't it be strange to see a thirty year old person still sitting in kindergarten? It wouldn't be natural.

Growth is natural. And Spiritual growth is natural for the child of God. However, many Christians don't grow, and the main cause of this lack of growth is desire. They don't desire growth, so they don't grow. Without an honest and strong desire there can't be any meaningful growth.

Still other Christians want to grow, but they experience much difficulty because of wrong motives. They want to grow because they feel it is expected of them. They feel peer pressure from their brothers and sisters in Christ, so they try to grow. They don't know about the rest that is theirs in Christ because they are too busy trying to grow. This can only lead one to frustration and despair.

What I'm sharing with you from the Song of Solomon is that spiritual growth, born out of a healthy desire for God, will be the delight of your life. There's no peer pressure involved here. There's just the knowledge of the sweet words of God, the pleasantness of being in the presence of your Beloved Friend; and this produces the desire for more. *"My companions are listening for your voice - let me hear it!"* Isn't that wonderful?

So, the first blessing for you, in hearing the voice of Christ, your Friend, is found in your ability to have a genuine desire to know Him and grow in Him.

THE BLESSING
OF JOY

In the Gospel of John, Chapter 3, verse 29, John the Baptist had this to say concerning Jesus: *"The friend of the bridegroom, who stands and hears him, rejoices greatly because of the bridegroom's voice. And so this joy of mine has been made full."* Once again, this verse ties together friendship with God and hearing God's voice.

Isn't it interesting, and significant, that once more Jesus is portrayed here as a bridegroom? You are His bride; He is your Bridegroom.

The most intimate relationship existing on earth is the marriage relationship. Two people cannot be bound any closer than in marriage. It's for this purpose that we see Jesus repeatedly depicted as our Bridegroom. He wants to get through to us just how close we are to Him. Hopefully, it is getting through to you, becoming clearer and clearer, as you read this book.

Look at John the Baptist's words. The situation behind this verse was that John's disciples were a little upset over the fact that Jesus was becoming bigger in reputation than John. They saw this as a threat to their ministry, or a type of rivalry between their ministries. They didn't have the larger picture of what God was doing. They could only see God's purpose as it pertained to them. So, they came to John and let him know their feelings about all this. John knew he had been ordained as the forerunner, as one crying in the wilderness, *"Make ready the way for the Lord"* (Matthew 3:3). And John knew Jesus was the prophesied One, the Lamb of God. Rather than being upset, or threatened by Jesus, John was filled with joy, for he was witnessing the unfolding of God's plan right before his eyes. So he said, *"The friend of the bridegroom,"* referring to himself as the friend, *"who stands and hears him, rejoices greatly because of the bridegroom's voice."*

You and I are the friend also in this verse. The friend who listens to the Bridegroom's voice has joy. This is the main truth declared in this verse.

Hopefully all Christians want joy. I frequently receive calls on my radio program from Christians who complain about not having any joy in their lives. The answer is very simple. If you truly want joy, then listen to your Friend. Of course, many have never thought of God as their Friend. As I said earlier, if you don't see God as your Friend, then communication with Him is going to be difficult.

God wants you to have joy. It's not God's will for a Christian to be always walking around with a long face, mourning over the joyless life he or she has. That's not God's will. God's will is for you to have joy *"unspeakable and full of glory"* (*1st Peter 1:8, King James*). Jesus said, *"These things I have spoken to you, that My joy may be in you, and that your joy may be made full"* (*John 15:11*).

Some may say, "I want God's joy. I've tried. But I don't seem to ever be able to get it." It's not a question of your getting it. It's a matter of God giving it. And that's just what He has done.

He has given His joy to you. His Word is clear on this subject. Take the time to stand and hear your Friend, as John the Baptist says, and your joy will be full.

One particular area of God's Word I think you will find yourself rejoicing in is concerning His promises. Maybe in the past, you would come across some really good promise in Scripture and think, "Oh, if only that were true. If only that were for me." Knowing now that God is your friend, I believe you will find yourself saying, "Hallelujah! That's for me!" and you'll have joy.

Prayer will become a joy. Communication with God will be a joy. You'll rejoice greatly because of the Bridegroom's voice. No longer will you say, "Well, I suppose I should pay my dues today and pray for a little bit." Prayer will be a joy. You'll find yourself breaking out in spontaneous times of praise and worship. Standing and hearing your Friend's voice fills you with the knowledge of God's great love and commitment to you, and that produces this joy I'm speaking of.

I have this happen to me frequently. I'll be in the middle of doing something and I begin to think of God's love for me. The next thing I know, I'm having a one-man worship service. It's exciting. The voice of God is good. It's full of sweetness.

John said, *"and so this joy of mine has been made full."* A full joy is what God offers you; not a part-time joy, but a full-time joy. And this joy will infect every part of your life. As we saw earlier, from Jesus' statement in John 15, He has spoken so that our joy may be made full *(verse 11)*. All we have to do is stand and listen to our Friend, sit in the garden as the Song of Solomon said, and we will personally and progressively be knowing this joy.

THE BLESSING OF COUNSEL

The third blessing which comes to you from hearing the voice of your Friend is found in the 27th chapter of Proverbs. Verse 9 says, *"Oil and perfume make the heart glad, so a man's counsel is sweet to his friend."*

Good counsel is a valuable commodity these days. It's pretty common to hear of someone paying more than $100 for an hourof counsel from a psychiatrist. And many times there is no counsel. What you may get instead is a mirror. You say something like, "I'm so mad at old so and so." The psychiatrist responds by saying, "You feel anger towards this person, don't you?" On it goes. Each statement you make elicits a similar response, all with the good intention of getting to the bottom of things in the hope that perhaps, through your understanding the situation, you will be able to "see the light."

This country abounds with counseling techniques. Some techniques enjoy popularity surges only to subside as the latest and newest trends become known. There is much running to and fro by people anxiously seeking answers to their inner problems.

There is a well known prophecy of the Messiah in the Book of Isaiah which says, *"For a child will be born to us, a son will be given to us, and the government will rest upon His shoulders; and His name will be called Wonderful Counselor, Mighty God, Eternal Father, Prince of Peace"* (9:6). The first name ascribed to our Messiah in this verse is *"Wonderful Counselor."*

Jesus is all of these things to us. He is our Mighty God. He is our Eternal Father. He is our Prince of Peace. Each of these titles is given to us for our benefit, so we might realize these qualities in God.

I am thankful Jesus is also our Wonderful Counselor. It's one thing to acknowledge Christ as your God; it's quite another to acknowledge Him as your Counselor. To say Jesus is your Counselor means you recognize His willingness to guide you each day as you walk in this life. He's not a God Who sits disinterestedly at the other end of the universe. He's your active Counselor. He's with you. He's not a silent partner. He's your Counselor. He's involved in your life.

If you were in a difficult situation and didn't know where to turn, whose advice would you be most inclined to place your trust in; your worst enemy, a total stranger, or your best friend? Whose advice would you be interested in? Certainly not your worst enemy for he would be prone to purposely give you the wrong counsel. And not a total stranger either for he wouldn't know you and therefore could not fully appreciate or understand your situation. But your best friend would be motivated by loving concern and would be able to give good solid counsel.

"A man's counsel is sweet to his friend." Perhaps the greatest benefit you will receive from hearing the voice of God will be the counsel He will give you as your Friend. You know it will be counsel you can rely upon, because He is your Best Friend.

Sometimes we have a tendency to run from God when the going gets tough. We may feel like we've let God down by encountering a problem we couldn't handle. So we run away.

That's what Jonah did *(Jonah 1)*. God said He was sending Jonah as a prophet to preach against Nineveh, the capital of the Assyrian Empire. Jonah didn't care too much for that word from God. He may have felt inadequate and not up the challenge. So he jumped on a boat and headed for Tarshish, in the opposite direction from Nineveh. God wasn't going to let go of Jonah though, so He whipped up a storm with the intention of Jonah repenting. Jonah knew the storm was from God but, instead of turning back to the Lord, in a fit of guilt he had himself thrown off the boat into the sea. He figured he had let God down and that was the end of it. If only he had known God as his Friend, he could have saved himself from a rather unpleasant trip back to the mainland. God didn't want Jonah to toss himself into the ocean. He wanted Jonah to return to Him.

May we learn not to run <u>from</u> God, but <u>to</u> God as we encounter life's difficulties. I think we can and will learn this if we will be diligent to see God as our Friend. If we will know Him as our Friend, we will want to receive His counsel, and it will be sweet to us.

You won't be too successful in following God if you don't know where you are going. The only way to know where to go is to have God's counsel. As you seek guidance from Him, you will find yourself walking in His Spirit. You will enjoy His fruitful and faithful words, and you will have the guidance you need. God's personal counsel for your life is the third blessing you will be knowing as you hear the voice of your Friend.

82

THE BLESSING OF
CORRECTION

This is the fourth blessing - correction. That doesn't sound too attractive at first, does it? "What kind of a blessing is that?" you may say. Correction doesn't sound as nice as having desire, joy, and counsel. One's initial conclusion may be that the word "correction" carries a negative connotation with it. If you need to be corrected, then that must mean you are wrong about something, and nobody likes to be wrong. If we had our way, we would always be right and never be wrong. Well, that's being a little idealistic, isn't it, because we are wrong sometimes. If we will be completely honest and transparent with ourselves, we will admit that we are wrong lots of times.

We are all people of opinions. There's something within us which makes us feel as if we have to have a solid opinion about everything. Many times, our opinions are based more upon ignorance than knowledge. If we truly knew all there was to know about a subject, we would probably have a different opinion than the one we have. But, because we have only limited knowledge, we form our opinions based upon what we do know. So, our opinions are based upon what we do know as well as upon what we do not know, and therein is our margin for error. As much as we hate to admit it, we are wrong an awful lot. Keeping this in mind, I think you will be able to look upon correction from the Lord as a blessing.

Here's a rather cryptic sounding Scripture from the Book of Proverbs: *"Better is an open rebuke than love that is concealed. Faithful are the wounds of a friend, but deceitful are the kisses of an enemy" (27:5-6).*

I'm the president of a non-profit organization, Loving Grace Ministries Inc. Every week we reach out with the Gospel through radio, tapes, literature, music, Bible courses, and more. As president, I have a number of people I employ who are crucial to this work. I am glad we are close enough that if someone disagrees with me about something they feel free enough to say so. I would hate it if I were completely surrounded by "yes men." You know, no matter what I would say, they would say, "Great idea, boss; that's right, Mr. Monbleau." There's not much honesty in that kind of a relationship, is there?

If you feel you can never disagree with someone because you are afraid about what they will think of you, then you don't have a close relationship with that person.

"Better is an open rebuke than love that is concealed." What is a rebuke? The Hebrew word for rebuke is "to-kay-khaw." It means: correction, chastisement, refutation. The truth

spoken in this verse is this - when you are in need of correction, it's better for someone to correct you than it is for someone to keep silent because they are afraid of hurting your feelings. A sign of a close friendship is when you know there is a deep enough love to endure a perhaps unpleasant chastisement. In this verse, to rebuke someone means you care enough to say something. The love that is concealed, or the love that remains silent, is actually a shallow love when compared to the type of love that is willing to speak out.

I have a little son, Jesse Francis Monbleau. If I saw him getting into something that might hurt him, like the utensil drawer, you better believe I would correct him pretty quick. I certainly wouldn't say, "Gee, I don't want to hurt his feelings. He might cry if I take that knife away from him." That would be ridiculous, wouldn't it?

Thank God that He cares enough about us, as His children, that He is willing to correct us. We have probably all been spared from harmful situations because our Lord cared enough to straighten us out when we needed it.

This sixth verse from Proverbs 27 is a rather mysterious sounding statement at first glance. *"Faithful are the wounds of a friend."* Upon close inspection, however, the meaning is clear. When God does rebuke us, it hurts. It's like a

85

wound. There is pain. But you see, it's a faithful wound. It's a wound that will produce growth. It's a wound that will spare you from a greater hurt in your life. It's a hurt that heals. Why does God do this? As this verse says, He does it because He's your Faithful Friend.

It's great to hear God's promises of victory and blessing to us. It's wonderful to see in Scripture how much God loves us. But it is just as important, and just as much a sign of love, to see God's Word correct us and rebuke us when we need it. Are you willing to see this as a blessing? It really is.

I praise God for the love He shows me, and I praise Him for caring enough to give me a sharp word of correction when I need it. Hebrews 12:11 says, *"All discipline for the moment seems not to be joyful, but sorrowful; yet to those who have been trained by it, afterwards it yields the peaceful fruit of righteousness."* Amen. That is the truth. Nobody likes correction at the moment it arrives, but afterwards we are thankful that someone, with greater wisdom than ours, took the time to discipline us.

The four blessings I've shared with you present a well-rounded picture of a healthy and vibrant relationship - a growing desire for God, a joy in the Lord, the knowledge of Christ as your Counselor, and the correction of the Lord. As we have seen, each of these blessings come directly as a result of your hearing God's voice, the voice of your Friend. What a tremendous and exciting blessing it is to know that you will be hearing His voice progressively clearer as you grow in your understanding of your friendship with God.

CHAPTER 5

PROTECTING YOUR FRIENDSHIP

Look out! Someone is out to undermine your friendship with God.

For the past four chapters we've looked at the importance of your friendship with God. We have seen how the understanding of your friendship with God is absolutely essential to the experience of living a truly abundant life in Christ. The knowledge of Jesus as your Friend, and yourself as His friend, is the cornerstone to abundant living. Without this awareness in your life, God's promises, plans, and purposes may seem elusive to you. Knowing where you stand with God, as His beloved friend, and hearing the voice of your beloved bridegroom, places you in the position to be able to receive and enjoy God's truth.

I think it would be a good idea to pause

right now in this discussion of your friendship with God to take a look at the fact that someone is going to try to deprive you of this great relationship you have been given with the Lord.

As Christians, we have an enemy. His name is Satan and he will do what he can to thwart the friendship that is yours with Jesus. You can be sure he will do his best or, perhaps I should say, he will do his worst to undermine at every turn your knowledge of your friendship with God. The devil knows that if you tap into this kind of relationship with God, you will be as strong and as fulfilled as you can possibly be. So, he will try to stop you. The purpose of this chapter is to show you what his devices are and how you can overcome the obstacles he will cast in your path.

First, let's take a brief look at some of the characteristic traits of our enemy. Then, I will share with you what I believe are Satan's four chief weapons against you regarding your friendship with God. As we look at each one, I will also show you, from Scripture, the way you can be free and triumphant over these weapons of the enemy.

KNOW THE DEVICES OF YOUR ENEMY

The apostle Peter wrote, *"Your adversary, the devil, prowls about like a roaring lion, seeking someone to devour"* (I Peter 5:8). If we know the tricks of the adversary, we will be able to steer clear of his snares. Satan can roar all he wants, but the Christian who is aware of his, or her, power in Jesus Christ will not be able to be devoured. Satan does want to devour you, but he can't because you belong to God. However, that won't stop him from trying and what he will try to do is make you think he can devour you. He knows if he can get you to swallow that lie, then you will be full of fear and your walk in the Lord will reflect that fear. Instead of being aware of God's power and love, you will be fearfully speculating about what the enemy might be up to next. So, the purpose of this section is to acquaint you with the truth of Scripture regarding your adversary, the devil. And, as our Savior said, *"You will know the truth, and the truth will make you free"* (John 8:32).

Psalm 3, verse 7 tells us, *"Thou hast shattered the teeth of the wicked."* As we look at Scripture together in this chapter, I hope you will see that behind that fierce roar of the wicked one is a mouth without teeth. It would be a true statement for the Christian, who knows the facts of Scripture, that Satan's roar is worse than his bite. God has shattered his teeth so don't let yourself be fooled by his roar.

In 2nd Corinthians 2:11, the apostle Paul wrote, *"in order that no advantage be taken of us by*

91

Satan; for we are not ignorant of his schemes." Translation: If you know the schemes of the devil, he won't be able to take advantage of you. Let us not be ignorant of his schemes. Instead let us know his devices so we may have a better walk with the Lord.

Perhaps I should mention a word of caution at this point. As Christians, we are called to *"fix our eyes on Jesus" (Hebrews 12:2)*. We are to walk through this life in a Christ-awareness, or Christ-consciousness. I mention this because I've seen many a Christian become engrossed in a devil-consciousness. It starts out innocently enough. A person may want to know the weapons of the enemy so they can be on guard against them, much like what I'm sharing with you now. But things take a turn for the worse if one becomes caught up in a morbid fascination with the devil. Instead of growing in the *"grace and knowledge of Jesus Christ" (2 Peter 3:18),* this person becomes completely captivated with the devil. I have a term for this. I call it "reverse bondage."

Here's what I mean by "reverse bondage." People who don't know Christ as their Savior live in the kingdom of darkness. Whether they know it or not this is, in fact, the kingdom they live in and they are in bondage to it. There's no human way out. It's only through receiving the sacrifice of Christ that one is able to be set free from the kingdom of darkness and become translated into the kingdom of Christ.

Some Christians, however, exchange their new found freedom for a different kind of bondage. Even though they may be proclaiming freedom in Jesus, and the defeat of the devil, they are still constantly thinking about the devil. They are constantly dwelling upon the snares of the enemy. I call this reverse bondage because, even though they claim to be victorious, they are still, nevertheless, captivated by a Satan-awareness.

We are not to become preoccupied with the devil. We are to walk in the Spirit in a Christ-awareness. Neither are we to be ignorant of the schemes of the devil, but we do have to be careful as to how to maintain proper perspective and priorities as Christians. As we go through this chapter, please keep this in mind. I want you to realize your victory over the devil so that, in doing so, you may experience true freedom and a conscious fullness in your relationship with Jesus Christ.

Let's take a look at what Scripture has to say about this enemy of ours.

Jesus called Satan the *"father of lies" (John 8:44)*. He also said the devil had come to *"steal, kill and destroy" (John 10:10)*. In Matthew 13:19 Jesus taught, in the Parable of the Sower, that Satan will try to steal God's Word from us.

93

I think we can see from just these three verses that we do need to be on guard. James wrote in his letter, *"Resist the devil and he will flee from you" (4:7).* Don't let Satan get between you and God concerning your friendship. Resist him, know his devices, know God's greater power, and he will have no choice but to flee from you.

There is one particular title given to Satan that I would like us to look at. In the twelfth chapter of the Book of Revelation, Satan is called the accuser of the brethren (verse 10). Did you know that Satan is out to accuse you? He'll call you names. He'll try to make you feel like a failure. He'll try to heap guilt and condemnation upon you. He'll point out your weaknesses and faults. He'll tell you God doesn't love you. He'll tell you that you don't really belong to God. In short, he'll accuse you in any way that he thinks will drive a wedge into your friendship with God.

The best way for you to combat these accusations is for you to know who you are in Jesus Christ. We have covered a lot of ground concerning this in the previous four chapters. I do hope you are seeing yourself in the Lord in a new and glorious way. Keep drinking in God's promises, and Satan's accusations will be of none effect.

Revelation 12:10 goes on to say, *"The*

accuser of our brethren has been thrown down, who accuses them before our God day and night." Boy, he doesn't give up, does he? Day and night he accuses us. Are you afraid of that? Does it worry you to think of Satan going before God and showering accusations down upon you? What do you suppose God says to all this?

VICTORY OVER
SATAN'S ACCUSATIONS

There is an example given in Scripture which explains God's reaction to Satan's accusations far better than I could ever explain it. It's found in the Book of Zechariah.

This text of Scripture says, *"Then he showed me Joshua the high priest standing before the angel of the Lord, and Satan standing at his right hand to accuse him. And the Lord said to Satan, 'The Lord rebuke you, Satan! Indeed, the Lord who has chosen Jerusalem rebuke you! Is this not a brand plucked from the fire?' Now Joshua was clothed with filthy garments and standing before the angel. And he spoke and said to those who were standing before him saying, 'Remove the filthy garments from him.' Again he said to him, 'See, I have taken your iniquity away from you and will clothe you with festal robes.' Then I said, 'Let them put a clean turban on his head.' So they put a clean turban on his head and clothed him with garments, while the angel of the Lord was standing by"* (Zechariah 3:1-5).

How does God respond to Satan's accusations? He rebukes him. He sends him away. And this is exactly what we should do whenever we sense the devil whispering his accusations in our ears. Don't even think about what he's saying. Resist him. Resist his words, and he will flee from you. It only makes sense that if God won't listen to Satan, then neither should we. God isn't interested in what Satan has to say about us. If Satan came before the Lord and said, "You know, God, that Wayne Monbleau character has some pretty bad faults," God could respond by saying, "Listen, I knew about all his faults and weaknesses before the world was even formed. I love him anyway. My Son died for his sins, and Wayne has accepted My forgiveness. I have cast all his sins into My sea of forgetfulness. I don't see those faults, Satan. All I see is a child washed in the blood of the Lamb and clothed with the garments of salvation and righteousness."

God could say that, but He doesn't even bother to explain it to Satan because He knows Satan knows these things. The devil knows I am clean in the Lord. Sometimes I think the devil knows these things better than we do.

Then why does he still accuse us? He does it because he doesn't want us to be seeing the truth of God's Word. Even though we are washed clean, he will try to make us feel dirty.

Even though it is a fact that we are forgiven, he will try to make us feel guilty. This is the whole reason why he accuses us. He is lying. He wants us to exchange the truth of God for a lie.

I love this passage of Scripture from Zechariah. Put yourself in Joshua's place. Here you are, and Satan is accusing you before the Lord. As you listen to what Satan says, you begin to feel filthy. You become aware of your sin and you feel dirty. Then God speaks. He rebukes Satan and sends him away. When that happens, you are no longer thinking about how dirty you feel. You are now able to see God clothing you with clean garments. And as verse 4 says, He has taken away your iniquity. You are clean! Can you see from these Scriptures how God looks at you? We need to see ourselves the same way God sees us. If we are willing to do that, we will learn how to effectively resist the devil. Don't accept the devil's filthy rags. Instead see yourself in the festal clothing of the Lord.

Do you want to know what my own favorite way is of resisting the devil? When I become aware of Satan trying to bother me, I start worshiping the Lord. I just completely disregard whatever Satan has to say, and instead I give praise to the Lord. You know what? When I am praising God, I find that Satan isn't around anymore. He's gone. He doesn't want to listen to me worship the Lord. In this way, I've discovered good can come out of the devil's accusations, because every time I sense him accusing me I say, "Well, it's time to have another worship service," and God and I have a great time together.

I used to try to fight Satan. You know, I'd get mad at him when I felt he was hassling me. I'd rebuke him and tell him to get lost. I think he enjoyed it when I told him to go away. It's hard, trying to fight the devil on your own willpower. It's not just hard, it's impossible. Then I began calling upon God and enjoying His presence; and for me, that's the best way I know to resist the devil. Fighting the devil is like staying in his territory, whereas I have found that worshiping God is like stepping up into His glorious higher ground.

Yes, we have got a tricky enemy. He will do what he can. So, let us be aware of his tactics and, when he tries to foul us up, we won't find ourselves falling for it. Let's go back to what Paul said, *"in order that no advantage be taken of us by Satan; for we are not ignorant of his schemes"* *(2 Corinthians 2:11)*. By knowing the schemes of the devil, we will be insuring that we won't be taken advantage of by any of them.

FOUR WEAPONS SATAN WILL USE
IN TRYING TO DESTROY
YOUR FRIENDSHIP WITH GOD

I'm going to share four weapons, or plots, of Satan's with you. I do this so the devil won't be able to gain any advantage over you at all regarding your friendship with God. If you are aware of these things, and if you keep watch in these areas, not only will you be sure not to get tangled up in the snares of the devil, but you will actually be strengthening your relationship with Jesus Christ. Remember, God wants to build a strong friendship with you. Anything trying to come in the way of this special relationship is not from the Lord.

REPEATING A
MATTER

Most of the Scriptures I will be sharing with you in this section are taken from the Book of Proverbs. Proverbs is a book full of the wisdom of God. It is, therefore, probably one of the most practical books in the Bible.

Satan's first weapon against you is described in the seventeenth chapter. Verse nine says, *"He who covers a transgression seeks love, but he who repeats a matter separates intimate friends."*

I want to divide this verse into two parts. Let's start by taking the first line. *"He who covers a transgression seeks love."* Do you know Who

99

this line refers to? It's God. Our good and loving Friend covers our transgressions because He is seeking love. He knows if you are seeing your transgressions, or sins, you won't be drinking in His love. Instead you'll be dwelling upon your failures. God is seeking your love. He covers your sins so you will be able to respond to His mercy and kindness by showing Him your love. That's what God is after: your love.

How sad it is that many believers have a narrow and limited concept that all God wants out of them is their service. It's as if one were to say, "It's not me that God is interested in. It's my works." That's so wrong! God loves you for who you are, and not for what He can get out of you. He seeks love.

Some friendships are based upon politics. Others are based upon business. But God's friendship with you is based upon love, and nothing but love. In the first chapter, I showed you the verse where Jesus said, *"Greater love has no one than this, that one lay down his life for his friends" (John 15:13)*. Never forget that, not even for a moment. This is the foundation of your relationship with the Lord - love.

God covers your transgressions because He seeks love. In the example I gave you from Zechariah, how did God cover Joshua's transgressions? He removed the filthy garments and

100

clothed him in new, clean garments. This is what covering our sins means. God has taken your sins away from you, and He then covers you with His forgiveness and righteousness.

Suppose I take a book and place it on a table in front of you. What do you see? - a book. Now suppose I place that book inside of a box. What do you see? - the book? No, the book is covered. You can't see the book anymore. All you can see is the box. When you cover an object, you no longer see the object. You see the covering.

This is what God intends for us to experience in this life. He covers our sins. What is it then that we should be seeing - our sin or His covering? The answer is clear, it's His covering that we should be seeing.

The next time you fall down and sin, if you will look at the covering and not the sin, you will find yourself getting up a lot quicker. You will find yourself having a deeper appreciation for God's covering. His forgiveness, grace, and mercy will shine forth to you like never before. As a result of all this, you will be expressing your love and gratitude to the Lord. And this is precisely what He desires.

The prophet Micah wrote, *"Yes, Thou wilt cast all their sins into the depths of the sea" (Micah 7:19)*. You can't get something covered much more than to have it covered by the sea. For years people were trying to find the Titanic and they couldn't because it was covered by the sea.

Try to visualize this: God has taken all of your sins and has placed them in an iron locker. He has secured the locker with a strong chain and He has tossed that locker into the very depths of the sea. Down and down it goes, finally landing on the bottom of the ocean. Can you see the locker anymore? No, and as a matter of fact, you couldn't see it even if you wanted to. All that's left is the sea, or His covering.

God wants you to know that He doesn't look at your sins. He's looking at the covering which He Himself has fashioned. The prophet Isaiah put it this way, *"Thou has cast all my sins behind Thy back" (Isaiah 38:17).*

By taking care of the sin issue, God knows you are now free to see His love. John wrote, *"If we confess our sins, He is faithful and righteous to forgive us our sins and to cleanse us from all unrighteousness" (1st John 1:9).* God forgives you of your sin, and then He cleanses you from it. We need to learn to cast our sins behind our back, just like God has.

I'm not talking about overlooking sin. Nor am I saying it doesn't matter if you sin. Of course it matters. We need to ask forgiveness and repent of our sins. But it is crucial to recognize the fact that God casts our sins behind His back, into the sea. We need to do the same. If we will, then we will be able to see His covering and not our sin.

Notice the tense of the word *"covers"* used in Proverbs 17:9. *"He who covers a transgression seeks love."* It's in the present tense. It's not "He who will cover" or "He who has covered," but *"He who covers."* I believe God purposely wrote it this way so we would see the ongoingness of His covering. His covering is there whenever we need it. No matter when you look at this verse, it will always be in the present tense.

I'm glad the writer of Proverbs placed this line before the line that says, *"But he who repeats a matter separates intimate friends."* Now that we know the truth of God covering our sin, we will be able to watch out for the one who would repeat a matter.

What do you suppose this line about repeating a matter means? The first part of the verse sets the tone, speaking on the subject of sin. So, who is this second line talking about? - Satan. God covers sin, Satan repeats sin. As this line says, Satan repeats sin in order to separate intimate friends.

Have you ever had this happen in your own life? You do something wrong. You commit a sin, you confess it to God and, as we have just seen, God covers it. Yet, that sin still stays in your mind. You have confessed it.

103

You've received forgiveness. You've done all you are supposed to do. But there it is, standing out in your mind. You can't seem to lose the memory, and therefore the guilt, of what you did.

This is nothing more than Satan repeating a matter. He takes that sin, dredges it up out of God's sea of forgetfulness, and sticks it back in your mind again. He wants you to be thinking about that sin, rather than thinking about God's forgiveness. God has covered your transgression, but Satan is saying, "You terrible sinner. Look what you did. And you call yourself a Christian." You see, Satan knows if he can put you in a state of sin-awareness, then that will hurt your friendship with God. Instead of feasting upon your Bread of Life, Jesus Christ, Satan will try to serve you stale leftovers. This is why the Scripture says: *"He who repeats a matter separates intimate friends."* By hanging that old sin in your mind, Satan is trying to separate you from your friendship with God.

You have got to understand that the accuser of the brethren will be constantly bringing up that which God has covered. Satan doesn't want you to be experiencing the joys of forgiveness and cleansing. He knows what a powerful weapon he has.

I'll tell you why this is such a powerful and effective weapon against the Christian.

Satan gets away with this trick so often because Christians think it must be God bringing the matter back up. Do you see what a sneaky enemy the devil is? He brings our sins back up to our mind, knowing we will think it must be God who is doing it.

Satan wants you to think God must be telling you to repent again, or to ask for forgiveness again. He wants you to think that God must really be mad at you. And, if you are not aware of the schemes of the devil, you just might drive yourself crazy trying to atone for your sin. Satan loves it when he sees a Christian thinking all this must be from God. Of course it hurts your friendship. You think God isn't pleased with you anymore. The sad result to all this is that once again, you find yourself captivated by a sin-consciousness rather than a Christ-consciousness.

God covers your sins. Satan repeats them. If you will remember these two simple statements, you will spare yourself from many agonizing times. Don't let the enemy use this evil weapon in his warfare against you.

I want you to do a simple exercise. The next time some sin from the past is brought up to you, regardless of whether it's a sin from years ago, or from a moment ago that you've just confessed; this is what I want you to do. Say, "God has covered that sin and I refuse to look at it. God is seeking my love and that is what I'm going to give Him right now. God has cast that transgression behind His back into the sea, and that's exactly what I have done too." By saying this, you won't even let Satan get a foothold. Don't even consider the sin. Let your heart, soul, and mind be filled with the knowledge of God's covering. Do this and you'll be able to cross off one of Satan's most powerful weapons. *"He who covers a transgression seeks love, but he who repeats a matter separates intimate friends."*

SLANDER

Once again, the text for this section is taken from the Book of Proverbs. *"A perverse man spreads strife, and a slanderer separates intimate friends"* *(16:28).* The portion of this verse I would like to concentrate on is *"a slanderer separates intimate friends."*

In the last verse, we saw Satan presented as one who repeats a matter. Now we see him as a slanderer, again with the intention of separating intimate friends. As I describe the ways in which Satan tries to slander, I believe you will be able to recognize times in your life when the devil has attempted to bring this weapon against you.

There are basically two ways in which the adversary slanders. The first is, He tries to slander God to us. The second is, He tries to slander us to ourselves. We will examine both of these tactics of his.

The devil will slander God to you. What do I mean by that? Satan will try to give you a distorted image of God. He'll try to make God appear as someone He is not.

Do you know what a "P.R." man is? "P.R." stands for public relations. It's the job of the public relations man to make his client appear in the best possible light. He wants the public to have a good image of his client.

Satan is just the opposite. He wants to make God appear in the worst possible light. He wants you to have a bad image of God. He will try to make you believe that God is cruel and vindictive. He wants to make you think that God is waiting to club you over the head. He'll tell you God is peering over His glasses, just waiting to let you have it. By allowing the enemy to slander God to you, you will wind up with a poor comprehension of the true nature of our Lord. Instead of seeing God's love and grace, you will be thinking He isn't pleased with you. Instead of experiencing abundant life, you will be afraid of life. The end result of this, once again, will be the separation of intimate friends.

If these are the types of images you carry in your heart about God, then let me tell you straight out; this is not from the Lord. God is love. In Him is life and His life is the light of men *(John 1:4)*. God is good.

God has come to be your intimate friend. He is not out to condemn you. Don't let Satan distort the true nature of the Lord. You will be able to guard against this best by actively drinking in the lovingkindness of God on a daily basis. By being intimately acquainted with what our Savior is really like, you will thwart Satan's attempts at slandering God to you.

"O taste and see that the Lord is good." That's the word from the 34th Psalm *(verse 8)*. Fix your eyes on Jesus and don't let anyone or anything take them off of Him. As the saying goes - if you've got the real thing, you'll be able to spot the counterfeit right away. The devil wants to, in effect, give you a counterfeit God and rob you of the real thing.

The second way Satan slanders is this: He slanders us to ourselves. In other words, He will try to make you look at yourself outside of Christ.

In Christ, you are a new creation *(2 Corinthians 5:17)*. In his first letter, John wrote, *"See how great a love the Father has bestowed on us, that we would be called children of God; and such we are" (1 John 3:1)*. As a new creation you have been given the ability to see yourself the way God sees you. This is a great privilege, a truly marvelous blessing. You can like yourself, because you are new. God has made you

108

someone special. You are free from the law of sin and death, and you are under the law of the spirit of life in Christ Jesus *(Romans 8:2)*. Inside Christ, you are beautiful. This is why the Bible says to lay aside the old nature and be clothed with the new *(Ephesians 4:22-24)*. God knows how important it is for your own spiritual well-being that you learn to see yourself as a new creation.

But old Satan will slander you and try to get you to look at yourself outside of Christ rather than in Christ. This ties in with the last Scripture I shared with you about repeating a matter. The devil delights in pointing out all of your faults and hang-ups. If you give him an opening, he will descend upon you with a constant barrage of criticisms and put-downs. He will attempt to hang all of your weaknesses in front of your eyes, hoping you will be seeing them rather than seeing your beautiful new nature.

If you are always talking about how un-worthy and sinful you are, you are actually just giving Satan an open invitation to do his thing on you. Some Christians have picked up this crazy idea that by making themselves look bad, they are somehow being "humble" and giving glory to God. It's not humility to be constantly looking at the doings of your old nature. That's not humility. That's self-abuse. God has called you to put on your new nature, to be consciously clothed with the knowledge of who He has made you to be in His love and forgiveness. You can't put on the new if you are always looking at the old.

Remember, God has covered your sins. It's not He who brings these matters up. It's Satan. God wants to reveal to you who you are in Him. The devil obviously does not want you to see who you are in Jesus Christ. He knows, if you do, you will be free of his slander weapon.

Be diligent to see and confess who your new self is. Learn to relate to your new nature, not your old nature. Do this and you will discover that the accuser of the brethren won't have any ground to stand on when he comes knocking on your door with his slanderous remarks.

Before we leave this passage of Scripture, I'd like to point out something. Have you noticed that both verses I've quoted from Proverbs refer to us as intimate friends of God? Proverbs 16:28 says, *"A slanderer separates intimate friends."* And Proverbs 17:9 says, *"He who repeats a matter separates intimate friends."* In both cases, the word *"intimate"* is used when describing the type of friendship Satan is out to break up.

Do you know what it means to be intimate friends with someone? It means to be so close that there are things shared between you and your friend which only you two know about. You are intimate. And that, my friends, is the type of relationship God has established with you - a beautiful, caring, intimate friendship.

I believe God wants to show you things He has never shown anyone else. God has little secrets which are just to be between you and Him. He wants to bring you into this intimate friendship. Maybe this seems too fantastic to accept, but I sincerely believe this with all my heart. I think this is exactly what Revelation 2:17 is trying to get across to us when Jesus said, *"To him who overcomes, to him I will give some of the hidden manna, and I will give him a white stone, and a new name written on the stone which none knows but he who receives it."*

According to this verse, there will only be two people who know your new name - you and God. Right?

Do you know what manna is? That's what God fed his people, Israel, while they were in the wilderness. When this verse from the book of Revelation speaks of *"hidden manna,"* I believe God is saying He has secret food that is just for you. God desires to open up gleams of riches to you that nobody else has ever seen in quite the same way. God has a uniquely intimate friendship for you.

After all, we are individuals. There are no

two of us exactly alike. This should tell us something about our Lord. He obviously has made us all as individuals, and He wants to relate to us as individuals.

We have been given an intimate friendship in Jesus Christ. God is a close and inseparable friend, and we have the privilege of progressively knowing Him this way every day.

SPIRITUAL POVERTY

Here is another way Satan will try to come against you. Proverbs 19:4 says, *"Wealth adds many friends, but a poor man is separated from his friend."* Again, the term "separated" appears. Satan repeatedly attempts to separate us from God. He can't in fact do this, but that won't stop him from trying to convince us that he can.

How do you see yourself in regard to spiritual riches? Do you know how rich you are in the Lord? In Ephesians 1:3, Paul wrote, *"Blessed be the God and Father of our Lord Jesus Christ, Who has blessed us with every spiritual blessing in the heavenly places in Christ."* That's *every* spiritual blessing! You and I are richer than either of us know. We have been given every single blessing existing in the heavenly places.

I don't know all of my riches yet, but that excites me. I look at each day as a new opportunity to discover more of my riches in Christ.

There is no end to our riches in the Lord. The knowledge of this gives me great joy along with an ever deepening appreciation of my Best Friend, Jesus. He's such a Good Friend, isn't He? He is always giving us presents, and He is delighted to do so. His constant giving is intended to create a thankful response upon our part, so we will want to give back to Him and keep that intimate friendship in the forefront of our consciousness.

"Wealth adds many friends." Through the realization of our wealth in Christ, we are enabled to understand a great deal about our friendship with God. We certainly haven't earned these spiritual riches. They are free gifts of His grace and they are an expression of God's love for us. Paul goes on, in Ephesians, to list some of these riches of ours: holiness, blame-lessness, adoption as sons, grace, redemption, forgiveness, an inheritance, salvation, and the Holy Spirit *(Ephesians 1:4-14)*. All of these riches are already ours in Jesus Christ.

There is more. Psalm 68:19 says, *"Blessed be the Lord, who daily loadeth us with benefits" (King James)*. Just imagine yourself going to God and being given a big pile of blessings! Every day! And no matter how often you go to Him, He always has more.

Do you want to know what I consider the greatest blessing to be? Him! He Himself is the greatest blessing. When we come to that point, then we really know how rich we are in Him.

Proverbs 19:4 continues, *"But a poor man is separated from his friend."* In light of this verse, what do you suppose Satan will try to do? He will try to keep you from seeing your riches in Christ. He will attempt to make you feel like you don't have anything. What will this do to your friendship with God? It may very well cause you to develop a grudge against God. You may feel as if you have been shortchanged. You may say, "God, Your Word says I'm supposed to have an abundant life in You. How come I don't see it? How come You're not giving it to me?"

A poor man is separated from his friend. In this case, it would not be God walking away from us. It would be us walking away from God, if we let Satan rob us of the knowledge of *"every spiritual blessing in the heavenly places in Christ."*

The devil is skillful, and he will play upon any self-pity lurking around in us if he has a chance. If you feel sorry for yourself, you can be sure the devil will be there agreeing with you. "You poor soul. God doesn't love you. I guess you are the one person God forgot all about. Everyone else is being blessed, but not you." Don't listen to that kind of talk.

Even though you are rich in Christ, Satan will try to make you think you don't have anything. The way to stop him cold on this one is for you to let the Lord daily load you with His benefits. The devil will come up to you and tell you how little you have. When he does, just say this, "I don't have any time to talk right now, because I'm too busy getting loads of spiritual riches from Jesus." I tell you, Satan will run in the opposite direction if you hit him with that one. He sure doesn't want to stick around to watch you seeing your spiritual riches in Christ.

And this brings us to Satan's fourth sneaky weapon against you in your friendship with God.

SUBSTITUTE RICHES

When Satan discovers he can't rob you of your spiritual riches, he'll turn around and try to bribe you with substitute riches. He will attempt to give you something in the hope that you will take your mind off of what is yours in Christ.

James had this to say in his letter, *"Whoever wishes to be a friend of the world makes himself an enemy of God"* (James 4:4). After all his other tricks have failed, Satan will resort to this weapon. He will try to lure you away from the Lord by enchanting you with the things of this world. If you let him get at you with this one, you will be fooled into thinking true happiness can be found outside of Christ.

We can see how the devil tried to do this with the Lord. Jesus said He had come to do His Father's will *(John 6:38)*. He would often slip away to a lonely place to commune with His heavenly Father *(Luke 5:16)*. His life was an expression of an intimate relationship with God. But in Matthew's Gospel, in the fourth chapter, Satan attempted to lure Jesus away from His Father's will.

After his first two tries had failed *("If You are the Son of God, command that these stones become bread"* and *"If You are the Son of God, throw yourself down"* [from the temple], *Matthew 4:3&6)*, Satan resorted to this last tactic: *"The devil took Him to a very high mountain and showed Him all the kingdoms of the world, and their glory; and he said to Him, 'All these things will I give You, if You fall down and worship me'"* *(Matthew 4:8-9)*. Satan hoped that the kingdoms of this world would be more attractive to Jesus than the intimate relationship He enjoyed with His Father. The devil sought to separate this heavenly spiritual friendship by introducing another friendship. A substitute friendship with the world was what Satan was offering Jesus.

What would you do if Satan offered you all the kingdoms of this world? Would you accept or would you turn him down? The riches of this world can be attractive all right.

Countless lives have ended in frustration and destruction as a result of seeking true happiness from the things of this world.

But true happiness is a quality of the heart. It's internal. All that this world has to offer is external. Only God can satisfy the inner longings of your spirit. Don't be fooled by Satan's offers of happiness apart from God.

Going back to this example from Matthew, *"Jesus said to him, 'Begone, Satan! For it is written, "You shall worship the Lord your God, and serve Him only."' Then the devil left him; and behold, angels came and began to minister to him"* (4:10-11).

Jesus knew better. Satan underestimated and could never fathom the total joy which exists in a relationship with God. He failed to understand that anything he would have to offer could never even remotely compare with what God gives us.

Jesus sent Satan packing. Satan had offered externals, and that's all he could offer. For he could never realize the internal and eternal peace of heart, found only in knowing God.

This encounter between Jesus and the devil has a beautiful ending, *"Angels came and began to minister to Him."* God meets all our needs, internal and external. He knows what we need, and even if it takes a special trip from the angels, that's what He will give us.

117

The way to steer clear of this final weapon from Satan is for you to know and love God so well that anything Satan offers will seem like rubbish by comparison. When the devil finally realizes he can't separate you from God, he will try to introduce a substitute friendship. If you let yourself *"know the love of Christ which surpasses knowledge" (Ephesians 3:19),* on a daily basis, you won't have any trouble at all seeing through this weapon of the adversary.

Know the weapons of the enemy and you will be completely free to enjoy your Best Friend. I would hate to think of my sharing these great truths with you about your friendship with God only to have you not see them because of the snares of the evil one. God has a friendship for you that is the most intimate relationship you will ever experience. Be aware of Satan's tricks and you will insure that he won't be able to deprive you of this great friendship.

CHAPTER 6

LOYALTY

If I were to ask you to sum up, in one word, the essence of friendship, what would you say? Is there one word, capturing the true meaning of friendship, which comes to your mind right away?

I know what I would say. Without a doubt, I think the word "loyalty" is what a true, in-depth friendship is all about. Any friendship existing without loyalty is not much of a friendship, as far as I'm concerned.

Through the Old Testament Prophet, Hosea, God declared, *"I delight in loyalty rather than sacrifice, and in the knowledge of God rather than burnt offerings" (Hosea 6:6).* You see, loyalty is a quality of the heart, something enduring which emanates from the core of one's being, whereas sacrifice is simply something that one does. It would be possible to offer a sacrifice and not have your heart in it at all. I'm sure many of the Israelites in Hosea's day were just like that. Their relationship with God had become a mere ritual to them. There was no longer any real meaning to their sacrifices. It had all become reduced to the superficial realm of obligation, and it didn't even come near to their hearts. Earlier in this word from Hosea, the Lord had said, *"Your loyalty is like a morning cloud and like the dew which goes away early" (6:4).* When God said, *"I desire loyalty,"* He was saying that it's always been the heart that He has been after. God has always desired an in-depth relationship with His people; not merely a "Sunday morning" superficial type of relationship.

Loyalty is a quality of our heart that God is looking for. In this chapter I will show you that loyalty is a quality of God's heart toward us. This is the essence of His friendship with us. His feeling for us as His friends goes deeper than any of us could ever possibly realize. As we look at God's loyalty I hope you will see, in an even greater way, the depth of His love for you.

There is a touching example from the Old Testament which shows us the blessing and bond between two loyal friends. I'm speaking of David and Jonathan.

Jonathan was King Saul's son and the next in line to be king. However, due to Saul's lack of loyalty to the Lord, David had been anointed king by the prophet Samuel. Wisely, David did not try to bring about his own kingship. He left things in God's hands and trusted in His timing.

David used to play his harp for Saul to soothe Saul's troubled spirit. Saul would get so blessed whenever David ministered to him. But there was one problem. Saul was insanely jealous of David, for David was becoming quite famous as a mighty man in Israel. He had slain Goliath and God's blessing was upon all David did. The people of Israel clearly loved David. There was a song the people sang that said, *"Saul has slain his thousands, and David his ten thousands"* *(1st Samuel 18:7)*. Saul didn't like that, and in fits of rage, he would try to kill David.

Even though this friction existed between Saul and David, it did not affect the deep friendship between Jonathan and David. They loved each other deeply. There's one verse in particular I want to share with you, but I encourage you to read this whole account for yourself in I Samuel, Chapters 17-20. You will see what a great love and commitment these two friends had toward each other.

In chapter 18 of 1st Samuel, the first verse says this: *"The soul of Jonathan was knit to the soul of David, and Jonathan loved him as himself."* Their souls were knit together. In other words, when it came to their hearts, they were inseparable. This describes the depth of our friendship with God. If we will have eyes to see and ears to hear, we will know this type of loyalty for ourselves for this is the depth of God's loyalty towards us. Loyalty helps us see that our soul has been knit together with God's.

In the New Testament, 2nd Corinthians 5:17 says we are *"in Christ,"* and Colossians 1:27 says Christ is in us. Now that's knit together! The more you dwell upon this truth, the more you will have a greater assurance concerning God's loyalty to you, and this will positively affect every aspect of your life. God has knit His soul to yours, and yours to His. Just as Scripture says, *"Jonathan loved him as himself"* so does God love you as Himself. I don't believe a relationship can go any deeper than that.

It would be impossible for God to be disloyal. I have shown you quite a bit about the nature of God in this book. He has initiated this friendship we have with Him, and as we have looked into these things, I hope you have seen many facets of His True Personality. For God to be disloyal would be a complete contradiction of all I know about Him and of all the Bible tells us. God is the epitome of loyalty.

God is not a fair-weather friend, here today and gone tomorrow. He is a Loyal Friend. We have looked a few times at Hebrews 13:5 which says, *"I will never desert you, not will I ever forsake you."* That's loyalty. And Hebrews 6:18 says, *"It is impossible for God to lie"* (Titus 1:2 also says this). This is why I believe God could never be disloyal. He has given us His Own Word concerning His love toward us, and He will never go back on it. This is a good definition of loyalty; one who pledges himself to you and never goes back on his word.

I want to look more deeply into God's loyalty towards us. In order to do this, I'd like to break loyalty down into three categories.

There are three words I think of which give me a well-rounded understanding of loyalty: faithfulness, love, and commitment. These are true hallmarks of loyalty and each of these words is used in Scripture to define God's friendship with us. Faithfulness, love, and commitment are the heart of loyalty.

FAITHFULNESS

In the book of The Lamentations of Jeremiah, the 23rd verse of Chapter 3 says of God, *"Great is Thy faithfulness."* If you will look for any length of time at the faithfulness of God, I believe you too will declare, *"Great is Thy faithfulness."* This is a characteristic of God's loyalty. Throughout the rest of your life, as you grow in Christ, you will be experiencing His great faithfulness to you in an ever-increasing way, and His faithfulness will shine especially when you are in your trials.

Deuteronomy 7:9 says, *"Know therefore that the Lord your God, He is God, the faithful God."* What kind of God is our God? He is *"the faithful God."* This is how He wanted His children, Israel, to know Him and this is how He desires you to know Him.

Of course, you can only experience the faithfulness of God in your own life as you grow day by day in Him. Faithfulness is a quality that you realize over a period of time. When you look back over the years and see how faithful God has been to you, this will only make you know, beyond any doubt at all, that His faithfulness is never ending.

Do you know Jesus as your Faithful God? Can you say to Him from the bottom of your heart, *"Great is Thy faithfulness"*? The Bible calls God faithful in at least 12 different places.* This is a quality of God which we have to be aware of if we are going to get anywhere in our understanding of the Lord.

*Deut. 7:9; 1st Cor. 1:9, 10:13; Ist Thess. 5:24; 2nd Thess. 3:3; 2nd Tim. 2:13; Heb. 2:17; 1st Peter 4:19; 1st John 1:9; Rev. 1:5, 3:14, 19:11.

How deep do you think God's faithfulness goes? To what extent would God be faithful? It's one thing to say with your mind, "Isn't it great that God is faithful?" But, it's something else to know, by way of experience, the depth of His faithfulness. The Bible makes a statement concerning this, one which may be almost too hard for some Christians to believe. But it's there in Scripture and I think the Apostle Paul must have purposely written it this way in order to shock people and make them think about it. He wrote, *"If we are faithless, He remains faithful" (2nd Timothy 2:13).* Can you accept that? If someone was faithless to you, would you remain faithful to them? This is the type of faithfulness that is found in loyalty. It's a faithfulness which is not dependent upon someone else.

All too often, we make the mistake of measuring God according to our standards. We know that if someone turned their back on us in our hour of need, we would be hurt and would probably give up on that person. So, we may unknowingly bring that thought right into our relationship with the Lord. We may assume God must be hurt and disappointed if we fall down or run out of faith. We may think that when we give up, He gives up.

It's just not true. *"If we are faithless, He remains faithful."* Don't make God so small.

125

Don't reduce Him down to your size. Let Him be as big as He really is. Great is His faithfulness. See? His faithfulness is much greater than you or I will ever know.

Do you know why God remains faithful? Why would God stay faithful, even if we were to be faithless? This whole verse from Paul's letter to Timothy says, *"If we are faithless, He remains faithful; for He cannot deny Himself."* I shared with you earlier that God cannot lie, and He did say He would never leave us. Nothing will ever change that. So, in that sense, He can't deny Himself, because He would have to deny His Word.

But there is something else here, too; something we truly need to see. Where is Jesus right now? The Bible says He is in you: *"Christ in you, the hope of glory"* *(Colossians 1:27).* I think this is what Paul meant when he wrote this verse to Timothy. If God were to stop being faithful to you, He would have to deny Himself, because He is in you. So obviously, He couldn't do that. He is in you! Do you see this? I know this may seem a little hard to believe for some, but I'm just showing you what the Word says. *"If we are faithless, He remains faithful; for He cannot deny Himself."*

There's one more thing I'd like you to think about regarding this verse. Where do we get our faith from, anyway? Is faith something we produce on our own? Is it just a case of our gritting our teeth and somehow faith appears? No, of course not. The faith which we have comes from God. *"Faith comes from hearing, and hearing by the word of Christ" (Romans 10:17).* So, if we became faithless, He remains faithful to us, so that we may once again gain faith from Him. He is the storehouse of our faith. Faith comes from Him, and He will never give up on you.

Isn't it a relief to know God remains faithful? Doesn't this truth make you want to love and praise the Lord all the more? No matter what you do, He remains faithful. The knowledge of this fact will only make you want to be even more faithful to Him in return. When you are truly touched by His great faithfulness, this will produce an even closer friendship, and your desire will be to walk with your Best Friend at all times. He is our faithful God.

LOVE

Love is a part of loyalty. Any form of loyalty that exists without love can't be a real heart-to-heart relationship.

Do you know what the difference is between a partnership and a relationship? A partnership is an agreement to work together for some purpose. There has to be a kind of loyalty in order for a partnership to succeed, but there doesn't have to be love. A partnership can exist very easily without love. Businesses want loyal employees to work for them. That's a financial partnership. You do this job and I'll pay you this amount. Does there have to be love in that partnership? No, not at all.

A relationship is different. A relationship is personal. It touches the heart. A partnership is external. A relationship goes inside. It's an internal matter. Can a marriage progress without love? No. Can a friendship grow without love? No. In a partnership, two or more people come to an agreement about an external goal. In a relationship, however, the goal is the heart.

How do you see yourself with God? Have you been living in a partnership when all along God has desired a relationship? If you don't know the answer, I have a simple test for you which will help you see where you are.

Answer this question: do you think more about what you must do for God, or about who you are in God? If you think more about what you must do for God, then I'm afraid you have chosen the partnership mentality. It's all on the outside. You think more about your actions than about your soul being knit to His. But, if your answer is you think more about who you are in God, then you are aware of your relationship. You know God desires your loyalty more than your sacrifice. Of course a relationship does manifest itself in action, but a partnership is only about action.

Yes, loyalty can exist without love, but it's a cheap loyalty. It's a surface loyalty, a contract loyalty. Hopefully, you will desire to know the beneath-the-surface loyalty God has for you. God has not called you to be His partner. He's called you to be His child. That's a relationship, and it's filled with love.

Proverbs 17:17 says, *"A friend loves at all times."* I believe this verse is speaking about God's love for us. His love is constant and His love is consistent. Jesus loves us all the time. *"Love never fails" (1st Corinthians 13:8).*

It is so important to know this. When you've had a day where everything has been great and you have enjoyed victory in Christ, it's not too difficult for you to agree with and to feel that God loves you. But what about the other days; the days where everything goes wrong and you may feel like a complete spiritual flop? This is when it is crucial for you to know that your Friend, Jesus, loves you at all times. Nothing will pull you out of that rut faster than the knowledge of God's love for you at all times. His love will lift you up, give you peace, and grant you strength and vision.

God loves you when you're on the mountain top of victory, and He loves you when you are in the valley of defeat. Whether you're mad, glad, or sad; God's love remains the same. Why? Because God's love is not dependent upon you. It's dependent upon Him. God's love is not based upon what you do, or who you are, or what you're like. His love is based upon His Own Nature, and because of that, He is able to love at all times.

I realize that with us it's different. Usually, the love we express is very much dependent upon outside responses. If someone hurts us, our love valve may turn off. If someone is good to us, our valve opens up. God is not like we are though. First John 4:16 says, *"God is love."* You see, love is not so much what God does as it is Who He is. God's very nature is love. Love is what He is, so He can't help but love at all times. That's the way He is. He is love.

God knows what you are like. He knows your good qualities and your faults. He knows your strengths and weaknesses. He knew all of this long before you ever knew Him. And do you know what? He loves you anyway. This love I'm talking about is a different kind of love than you will find anywhere else. It's God-love, and it runs deeper and is more loyal than any other love in the world. The first verse of Scripture I ever learned as a Christian was John 3:16 which says, *"God so loved the world, that He gave His only begotten Son."* That's the depth of His love.

Jeremiah 31:3 tells us what kind of love God has for us. The Lord said, *"I have loved you with an everlasting love; therefore I have drawn you with lovingkindness."* God's love lasts forever; it never runs out. Because God's love is a forever love, we can have confidence in it. He has drawn us to Himself with lovingkindness. The very fact of your knowing Jesus Christ as Savior in the first place is the result of His love having already touched you. If you have any love in your heart at all for God, it is there because of His love for you. John wrote, *"We love, because He first loved us" (1st John 4:19).* That's everlasting love. Any love we have toward God has actually been produced through His love for us.

We really must stop placing limitations upon God's love. Instead, we need to ask Him to open our eyes and ears to see and hear the truth of His love. God loves us at all times. His love is an everlasting love. He is love, and we love because He first loved us. Let us open our hearts to Him so that the magnitude of these truths may be ever more meaningful to us.

Do you believe that no matter what shape you are in, God still loves you? It seems that sometimes we are so afraid to make so bold a declaration, and yet I find in my own life that the acceptance of this great truth is what produces a desire in me to grow and obey the

Lord. All too often we put things in reverse. We think that if we obey, then He will love us. Walking in that frame of mind will only produce frustration and disappointment, because we unknowingly make God's love dependent upon us. As I shared earlier, that's not the way it is. It's by receiving His love on a daily basis that we are able to obey. We love <u>because</u> He first loved us.

What came first, your action or God's action? It was God's action, wasn't it? Apply this truth now to your obedience. You obey, because He first loved you. If you try to obey on your own, you are the one producing obedience. If you receive God's love first, He will produce the obedience. Who do you suppose can do a better job when it comes to producing obedience, you or God? I hope the answer is obvious. The simple truth of your walk in the Lord is this: God's action produces your reaction. This is why it's so important to realize He loves you at all times, no matter what shape you are in.

Paul wrote, *"God demonstrates His own love toward us, in that while we were yet sinners, Christ died for us" (Romans 5:8).* Do you see this? Isn't this fantastic? God revealed His love by doing something for you long before you were able to do anything for Him. This a great principle. Even while you were a sinner, apart from God,

He loved you. You came into salvation by responding to what He had already done. Your reception of His action, or your reaction to His action, produced new life, and this is the way He intends for you to grow as a Christian. As you remain receptive to His love, it will always produce a response in your heart, and following Him will be your delight and joy.

Instead of feeling guilty when you are down, I encourage you to receive His love. This will produce in you the response you need and you will be lifted out of your valley. If you become depressed or feel defeated, the worst thing you can do is to imagine that God is displeased with you. That will only compound your problem. The reality is, God loves you in those moments just as much as He loves you in your times of victory. Again, the reception of God's action of love will produce in you the reaction of love you need.

Let me show you a Scripture which further illustrates this point. In the 14th chapter of Hosea, God was speaking to the backslider. A backslider is someone who knows God and His will, but falls away from following God. A backslider, or a person in a state of apostasy, consciously disobeys God. How do you suppose God feels about a backslider? In verse 4, the Lord said, *"I will heal their apostasy, I will love them freely."* Even in this case, which is about as extreme as you could get, God's love remains everlasting. How does a person come out of this condition? It's not just a matter of changing one's ways. Rather, it's about once again seeing and receiving the great love that God loves us with. The more you look at this truth the more sense it will make that, in fact, our entire lives are really just a matter of our responding to God's love.

I have counseled with many Christians who have lapsed into a backslidden condition. Without exception, the reason why they have remained in this state is because they feel they have let God down. They feel He no longer wants anything to do with them. Unfortunately, many times they've gotten this impression because they have experienced rejection from their own brothers and sisters in Christ.

You can imagine what happens when I share with them that God wants to heal their backsliding and love them freely. They respond! God's action of love produces their reaction, and once again they are experiencing the joy of fellowship with the Lord. It's like what Paul wrote to the Romans, *"The kindness of God leads you to repentance" (Romans 2:4).*

I am purposely belaboring this point because I feel it is so important, and so neglected. God's action produces our reaction. As you accept this truth, you will come to know His love as you should know it. *"A friend loves at all times."* Let God's loyal love take up residence in your heart, and you will never again be the same.

COMMITMENT

I came upon a quote a few years ago which I would like to share with you now. Back in the days of ancient Greece there was a politician and philosopher named Namertes. A wise and respected man, Namertes was held in high esteem by all the people. The story goes: "Namertes was on an embassy, when one told him, he was a happy man in having so many friends and asked him if he knew any certain way to try whether a man had many real friends or not. Namertes replied, 'Adversity.'"

Namertes had wisdom. He knew it was easy to have friends when all is well or when you are riding on the crest of popularity. But it's when the winds of adversity blow that you find out pretty quickly who your real friends are.

Commitment is the third word describing God's loyalty to us as friends. Jesus is committed to us. Whether we are in adversity or not, He is there. He has committed Himself to us. And it's in our times of trial that we may appreciate Him the most. All may forsake us but He will never leave us *(Hebrews 13:5)*.

Here is one of God's great promises of

commitment to you. In the Book of Isaiah, the Lord said, *"When you pass through the waters, I will be with you; and through the rivers, they will not overflow you. When you walk through the fire, you will not be scorched, nor will the flame burn you"* (43:2). Waters and rivers speak of problems in our lives which threaten to overwhelm us. Fire is representative of the tribulations we experience as God's children.

There are two great promises in this verse. The first is that these trials will not consume us - God will bring us through them. The second and perhaps greater promise is, God Himself will be with us through all these times.

Nobody likes fiery trials. I know I don't. But knowing God's presence in them can mean the difference between defeat and victory. As the beginning of this verse says, we're just passing through. If we were to think God would not be with us in these times of adversity, I'm sure we would wonder if we were going to make it through them. However, knowing His committed presence grants us the vision to know we will be all right. He is with us in any and all trials and tribulations. He is a completely committed Friend.

God tells us why He will be with us in these times of flood and fire in our lives. In the 4th verse from this passage in Isaiah God declares, *"since you are precious in My sight, since you are honored and I love you."*

God's attitude is not that He thinks He is doing us any special favors. Rather it's that we are precious to Him. He loves us, and that's why He is with us at all times. He could never possibly think of deserting us in any difficulty. On the contrary, it's in those moments that He wants to be the closest to us, because we are so precious to Him.

Proverbs 18:24 puts it this way, *"There is a friend who sticks closer than a brother."* You can't be any more committed than that. I believe Jesus is the Friend being spoken of here. He is closer to us than our own flesh-and-blood families.

You have probably heard the saying, "Blood is thicker than water." This is used in reference to the fact that, when the going gets rough, family ties are greater than bonds we have with others. I want to try a new saying out on you, based upon this verse from Proverbs. "Redeeming blood is thicker than family blood." That's really what this verse from Proverbs is saying concerning Jesus Christ's commitment to you. His commitment runs deeper than any family commitment could ever go. God is your *"Friend Who sticks closer than a brother."*

The Hebrew word for friend in this verse also means lover. In Young's Literal Translation of the Bible, the verse actually reads this way, *"There is a lover adhering more than a brother."* Again, your friendship with God is that intimate. He is your Friend and Lover. His loyalty and commitment to you are that intense.

Usually, even if all those we know fail us, we know we can count on our family to support us in our time of need. But even if your family were to give up on you, Jesus is there, sticking closer than a brother and ready to be your *"help in time of need" (Hebrews 4:16).*

By personally knowing God's commitment to you, you will be able to have the power you need over adversity. This truth is expressed beautifully by Moses in the Book of Deuteronomy. At this point in his life Moses was 120 years old and near the time of his death. He knew he would not be entering the land of Canaan, so he gathered the people of Israel together and spoke to them. He told them he would not be going with them into the promised land. He then encouraged the people by declaring to them that God would go before them into Canaan, conquering their enemies. Then he said, *"Be strong and courageous, do not be afraid or tremble at them, for the Lord your God is the one who goes with you. He will not fail you or forsake you" (31:6).* Moses knew, if his people would realize God's presence and commitment to them, they would have courage, they would be strong and they would not be overcome with fear. To make sure they understood this, he again stated, two verses later, *"The Lord is the one who goes ahead of you, He will be with you. He will not fail you or forsake you. Do not fear or be dismayed" (verse 8).*

There is One who goes before you, conquering your enemies. He will never fail you or forsake you. He will always be with you. Because of that, you can be strong and courageous. I'm not talking about strength in the flesh. I'm talking about a strength and confidence which is produced by the knowledge of God's committed presence in your life.

Do you know these truths? When you go into a battle, do you know you're not alone?

I dare say none of us fully appreciates how very precious we are to the Lord. We are more precious to God than anything else. He has taken an oath of loyalty to us. He remains faithful even when we are faithless. He loves at all times, and He sticks closer than a brother. This is loyalty in its truest essence. You will never find a loyalty greater than the loyalty God has toward you.

COMPLETE LOYALTY

Let me take a moment to show you what the word "friend" means in the biblical languages. The Greek word used for friend in the New Testament is "phelos," which means: to be a friend, to be fond of, to be dear to someone. Phelos means a lot more than just a casual acquaintance. Phelos speaks of an in-depth, loving friendship.

There are principally two words in the Hebrew language which are used for the word friend. One is "ahab," meaning: to have affection for, to love, to like, to be a friend to. The other word is "rayea," which means: a close associate, a brother or a companion.

The biblical concept of friendship runs deeper than our western civilization understanding of friendship. In the Bible, a friend is someone dear to you, someone you love from the depths of your innermost being. There's a bond of loyalty in biblical friendship that almost goes without saying.

In closing, I would like to share with you what I consider to be a most striking example of God's loyalty. At the beginning of this chapter, I told you I didn't believe God knew how to be disloyal. Maybe this statement surprised you. However, this Scripture I'm about to share with you from the Gospel of Matthew is why I believe this. In the life of Jesus, our Best Friend, we will see how complete God's loyalty is toward us. It surpasses anything you or I could ever comprehend.

This passage comes from the 26th chapter

of Matthew. It's about the night of Jesus' arrest in the garden of Gethsemane. *"And while He was still speaking, behold, Judas, one of the twelve, came up, accompanied by a great multitude with swords and clubs, from the chief priests and elders of the people. Now he who was betraying Him gave them a sign, saying, 'Whomever I shall kiss, He is the one; seize Him.' And immediately he came to Jesus and said, 'Hail, Rabbi;' and kissed Him. And Jesus said to him, 'Friend, do what you have come for.' Then they came and laid hands on Jesus and seized Him"* (Verses 47-50).

In the very act of betrayal, by one of His own disciples whom He had spent three years with, Jesus still referred to Judas as His friend. He called Judas His "phelos," one who is dear. Jesus did this because He didn't know how to be disloyal. It's just not in His nature. So, even in this situation, Jesus could only respond by calling Judas friend.

In essence, Jesus was saying, "Judas, you may betray Me and you may not consider Me as your friend, but I will never betray you." Judas wouldn't receive that, and later on he killed himself. I think this is expressive of the fact that Judas wouldn't accept God's forgiveness. He was overcome by guilt after he betrayed Jesus, but he obviously did not know Jesus' depth of loyalty and forgiveness, so he killed himself.

Jesus wasn't being sarcastic when He referred to Judas as friend. This was His genuine heart affection. As we've already seen, God cannot lie. God is loyal, and if you look at His loyalty long enough, Jesus' response in this portion of Scripture will make perfect sense to you.

God will never be disloyal to you. He can't be. In the same way that it is impossible for Him to lie, it is also impossible for Him to be disloyal.

Let's face it, you have found a Friend for life. The work which He has begun in you, He will complete *(Philippians 1:6)*. He will never leave you. He will always love you deeply and committedly.

Whether you're down, up, happy, overwhelmed with problems, or whatever, it won't ever change the way God feels about you.

Your understanding of Christ's loyalty to you is the cement in your friendship with God. Allow the Holy Spirit to minister this to your heart. You will discover joy in unexpected places. You will find goodness and love, where normally there would be none, as you grow in your great friendship with God.

Are you God's friend? That's the question I asked way back in the first chapter of this book. I really do hope your answer, regardless of what it was before, is now, "Yes. Praise God, He is my very Best Friend and nothing will ever change that."

My purpose in writing this book has been to send a love letter from Jesus to you. Step out into the glorious sunshine of your friendship with God. Go forth now and let no man separate what God has joined together.

May the peace of God, the joy of the Holy Spirit, and the faithful, committed, loyal love of your Savior be present and increasing in your heart every day. Praise Him and be eternally grateful for your friendship with God.